MW00719049

GREENGROCER'S
GUIDE TO THE
HARVEST

GREENGROCER'S
GUIDE TO THE
HARVEST

Curtis G. Aikens

PEACHTREE PUBLISHERS, LTD.
Atlanta

Published by
PEACHTREE PUBLISHERS, LTD.
494 Armour Circle, NE
Atlanta, Georgia 30324

© 1991 Curtis G. Aikens

All rights reserved. No part of this book may be reproduced in any form
or by any means without the prior written permission of the Publisher,
excepting brief quotes in connection with reviews, written
specifically for inclusion in a magazine or newspaper.

Manufactured in the United States of America
10 9 8 7 6 5 4 3 2 1

Cover and book design by Candace J. Magee
Composition by Kathryn D. Mothershed
Cover photo by Mike Moreland

Library of Congress Cataloging in Publication Data

Aikens, Curtis G.
Greengrocer's guide to the harvest / Curtis G. Aikens.
p. cm.
Includes index.
ISBN 1-56145-052-9 (trade paper)
1. Fruit. 2. Vegetables. 3. Nuts. 4. Cookery (Fruit)
5. Cookery (Vegetables) 6. Cookery (Nuts) I. Title
TX558.F7A37 1991

635—dc20

90-28259
CIP

To my parents, Laura B. Aikens and Eddie James Aikens, Sr., who will celebrate their fortieth anniversary May 12, 1991. Thank you for all your love and support—and thanks for the strength. I hope I make you both proud.

and

Dr. Martin Luther King, Jr.—whose life's work and dreams have allowed me to work and make my dreams come true.

Acknowledgments

This book would not be possible if hundreds of produce people in San Francisco, Oakland, New York, Atlanta, and other parts of the country had not been free with their knowledge and taught me their secrets to choosing fresh fruits and vegetables.

A very special thank you to the Marin County California Library and your literacy program, and especially to Jeni Hartman and Steve Seybold. I owe you a debt I doubt I can ever repay. Please keep teaching adults to read.

The editors of *The Rockdale Citizen*, Fred Turner and Tom Barry, for giving me a chance to write (and paying me!). Jack Lease, vice-president of WXIA-TV Atlanta, for caring about me and giving me a forum to share my knowledge of produce throughout the South.

Ruth Farmer, Margret Aikens, and Eileen Wischussen for correcting my spelling and putting up with all my mess.

Last, but certainly not least, Peachtree Publishers, old and new.

Contents

VEGETABLES

HERBS

NUTS

RECIPES

Introduction

Becoming a Better Greengrocer

When I broke into the produce business way back when, I thought I knew everything there was to know about fresh fruits and vegetables. You see, as a little boy, I was always around produce. My grandfather, W. H. Curtis, Sr., was the best farmer I ever saw, which brings me to the first term I would like to talk about—organic. Granddaddy, like most of the old timers, farmed organically long before we knew of nitrate leaching into our soil, the potential effects of alar, and pesticide residues. Granddaddy thought the old way was the best way. I can remember him saying, "I've seen lots of collard greens grown with bag fertilizer, but I ain't never seen any as good as mine, and I know they don't taste better." My dictionary says organically grown means using fertilizer and mulches consisting only of animal or vegetable matter with no chemical fertilizers or pesticides. That's the way Granddaddy did it, and he did it cost effectively.

With that in mind, when shopping for organic fruits and vegetables, never settle for limp dried looking produce—demand top quality, fresh and alive looking produce. If an organic retailer tells you the produce looks bad because the farmer can't use pesticides, then you politely inform him his supplier isn't much of an organic farmer.

One more Granddaddy story: He used to apply a white, milky-looking liquid to his garden. He didn't have a fancy name for it. He just referred to it as a lime mix. Nowadays, it is called Bordeaux, which is making a strong impact on the modern organic farmers.

The next few terms you may never see listed in the produce section or featured in any written advertisements, but knowing them and what they stand for will help you select fresher and sweeter produce, and this knowledge will also save you money.

When I started to shop for wholesale produce, I thought an apple was an apple; a mushroom a mushroom; and a zucchini, a zucchini. I had no idea a single produce item could be graded into one or no less than four categories. "Extra fancy" is the highest grade, then "fancy," "choice," and finally "mature," sometimes referred to as "number two." I learned those categories and what they stood for relatively quickly, thanks to people like Joe Carcione, Pat Murphy, and Charlie Bettencourt. All were men that I knew while buying in the Golden Gate Produce Terminal in south San Francisco. Each of them separately took me under his wing and shared his knowledge of the produce world. Before that, I would buy what I thought was top grade, later to find out I should have paid much less for that item. The following grade levels are not USDA standards. They are trade terms that the men and women of the produce industry have come up with over the years when discussing size, color, and quality of fresh fruits and vegetables among themselves.

Going from bottom to top, we'll start with **mature**. A good produce person will never say he has some bad produce to sell; however, he will say, for instance, "I have some number two mushrooms, or soup tomatoes I'm sure you could put to use." Remember, just because these items are our lowest grade does not mean the produce is bad or inedible. For example, number two mushrooms should not always be passed by. These mushrooms are mature and full-flavored, which makes them excellent for sauces and on pizzas. The soup tomato is another mature item that is too soft for sandwiches but excellent in soup and other cooked dishes.

The next produce grade level is **choice.** Vegetables with this grade level are usually considered irregular, be it size or shape; however, the taste is normally as good as any of the top grades. Fruits with this grade usually show slight blemishes. For the consumer on a close budget, the choice items could be your best shopping value.

The top two grades, **fancy** and **extra fancy,** are very hard to tell apart in fruits. With apples, for instance, an extra fancy apple shows 90 to 100 percent color. In other words, a red apple is completely red or close to it. Fancy apples show 75 to 90 percent color, although the taste is virtually the same. But the price could range from a ten to twenty cents per pound difference.

Now in vegetables, these grades of fancy and extra fancy usually stand for size, fancy being medium-sized; I'll use a zucchini for our measuring stick. A fancy would be six to eight inches long and from one and one-half to two inches around and extra fancy, four to six inches long and no more than an inch and one-half around. Small vegetables usually bring much higher price tags in most markets. However, taste does not vary much in fancy and extra fancy vegetables.

Now that you are familiar with some of the produce industry's inside grade levels and what they mean, I want you to know what I think are the four keys needed to unlock the door to becoming an expert greengrocer. These keys should guide you through any produce section, helping you choose the freshest and sweetest fruits and vegetables any greengrocer offers. One or more of these keys will always come into play in selecting fresh fruits or vegetables.

(1) LOOK. What I mean is always look at your fresh fruit or vegetable to be sure it has good color. However, color is not always a true indication of ripeness. The main things to look for are bruises or scars. If either is present disregard that item and choose one free from damage. Why? Let's face it. Pesticides and other chemicals are with us, but in most instances they are applied to the outside of produce. Therefore, if it can't be washed away, it can be peeled away. If scars or bruises are present, that pesticide on the outside may seep into the flesh of your fresh fruit item. So remember, avoid damaged produce.

(2) SMELL. Don't be afraid to follow your nose. Here is something I will never forget. Once while shopping in New York's Hunts Point Market, two so-called produce experts laughed at me for smelling tomatoes. I not only got upset, I got mad. I pointed out to those guys the boxes I did not select were bad. If they would smell they could tell. I also pointed out to the "experts" that as tomatoes ripen, they do give off a rather strong tomato aroma. Which brings up another good saying about fruits: If it *smells* peachy, it's going to *taste* peachy. Remember, as fruit ripens not only does the sugar level rise, the fragrance becomes much stronger and fruity. As for vegetables, when they pass their peak, they usually give off a slightly sour smell.

(3) TOUCH. No buyer of fresh fruit wants items that are either rock-hard or marshmallow soft. Most fruit when ripe gives just a little to slight pressure. Something I want you to remember—yes, it's okay to pick up produce and inspect it before buying, but please do not squeeze the life out of items, especially ones that you are not going to purchase. Remember, that piece of fruit that was too hard or too soft for your liking may be just perfect for someone else. Vegetables, be they broccoli, cabbage, carrots, or whatever, should always be firm. Never buy limp vegetables.

(4) SEASON. Know the season of fresh fruits and vegetables and buy what is in season. The seasons you will learn while reading this book. The buying part is up to you. However, each year this point gets more and more difficult to distinguish. With the ever-increasing shipments of fresh fruits and vegetables from the lower hemisphere, where the seasons are the opposite of ours. Before buying an item from a region with a reverse season, first see what that region has to offer.

One easy way to tell what is in season is to take a moment to look around your greengrocer's store or produce section of your supermarket and see which items are in the greatest abundance.

I guess I should add one fifth key—get to know your greengrocer, for he or she should be able to tell you anything about the produce in their shop. And if they can't, find a new greengrocer.

One further note: Although fresh fruits and vegetables will often keep a week in the refrigerator, it is best to use them within three days of purchasing. And in most cases, storing them in paper bags is preferable to storing in plastic ones.

Wax Coating on Produce

There is nothing new about waxing fresh produce. Most people don't realize that the first coating is applied by Mother Nature herself to protect the produce against hot sunlight and to retain moisture. Even when shopping for true organic produce, you may notice a fine layer of wax present on fruits and vegetables. You need not worry; that wax is a sign of freshness. The only way to get fresher produce would be to pick it from the garden yourself.

As for humans waxing produce, there's nothing new about that either. The Chinese have been waxing fruits for hundreds of years. For most of the twentieth century in America, processing houses have coated various produce items with a petroleum-based wax (with FDA approval), with waxing ranging from very fine on fruits like apples and grapes to quite thick on certain root vegetables like rutabagas, turnips, and some beets.

Nature applies wax to produce for protection; humans do so to enhance appearance and, more importantly, to extend the shelf life of fruits and vegetables. Waxed produce is the main reason I advise against buying bruised fruits. As long as the fruit is undamaged, the wax is confined to the skin and can be removed, but if the item is bruised, the wax may seep into the flesh and in turn be consumed by you or your children. Remember, the wax is FDA approved, but if you are like me, you want to be careful about how much petroleum-based product you have floating around inside your body.

How can you remove wax from produce? Neither natural nor artificial wax can be rinsed off in cold water, but nature's coating will evaporate on its own, and man-made wax can be removed in very warm water. However, the best way to ensure that no wax is consumed is to peel the produce. Don't stop buying fresh fruits because of waxing.

Harvest Guide

Fruits
Vegetables
Herbs
Nuts

FRUITS

FRUITS

Apples

Once the forbidden fruit, the apple is now the most pre-ferred. There have been more than seven thousand varieties documented since Adam took the first bite in the Garden of Eden. Out of those many varieties, the best-known and best-selling of all time is the **Red Delicious**. It's the perfect-looking apple, beautiful in color and quite shapely, and it has a nice, sweet flavor. However, although no other apple may be as pretty as the Red Delicious, you can find many other varieties with far superior flavor.

Starting with the green varieties, there are two that stand out in my mind and on my tastebuds. While living in northern California I was invited to a wine and cheese tasting out in the Napa Valley. The wine was good, but what caught my atten-tion was the apple being served on the cheese tray. No one at the tasting could tell me the name of the little green tomato-shaped apple until I found the gardener, who took me out to the orchard. He said the apple was a Pippin and that it's much better for cooking than eating out of hand. I found that hard to believe until I made my mom's apple pie using the Pippin. Here's that recipe if you would like to try it (you can use any apple to make her pie).

MOM'S EASY APPLE PIE:

Ingredients:

3-4 med. apples peeled, cored, and sliced
1 cup sugar
1/4 tsp. nutmeg
1/2 stick margarine
1 homemade pie crust

Instructions:

To crust add apple; pour sugar and nutmeg
over apples; slice margarine and arrange in pan;
cover with sheet of dough and prick in several
places; bake for 45 to 55 min. at 375 degrees.

The **Pippin** apple may be hard to find on the East Coast, but if you can find it, try it.

The other green apple I love is the **Granny Smith.** Each year this apple takes more and more of the American market than any apple since the Red Delicious. By the year 2000 the Granny Smith may be the world's most popular apple. These apples are light green in color and when fully ripened have a yellow tint up near the stem end. This apple is crisp to bite and has a tart, sweet flavor. I love the Granny Smith apple.

Another good apple is the **McIntosh:** this apple can't decide whether it's red or green, so let's call it two-toned. The McIntosh is juicy and tender, not too sweet, but sweet enough. The flesh is snow-white and makes nice applesauce. The McIntosh is probably the second best baking apple.

The best apple to bake is the **Rome Beauty.** This big boy can take the heat in the oven and won't collapse or lose its shape. Some experts describe this apple as having very little flavor, but I, on the other hand, truly enjoy its taste, which is faintly sweet, and one of the things I love about Romes is that they are very crunchy to bite.

Other apples you may want to try include:

Winesap: Growers aren't producing as many Winesaps as in years past. This is a mystery to me because this firm, dark red-skinned, yellow-fleshed apple is sweet, with a flavor that reminds me of homemade wine.

Mutsu: Imported from Japan, some say this is the perfect apple; it is crisp, juicy, and very sweet. The Mutsu sometimes grows to be as large as a melon. It is now being grown on the West Coast and is being marketed under the name *Fuji Apple.* I am sure this apple will become quite popular before long.

Rhode Island Greenie: For you pie makers, this is the best to use. It is tough to get, but if you want the best for your family, and if you take the time to bake homemade pies, cook with this apple.

Other apples that are hard to find, but worth the hunt are *Johnarhana* red apples, grown in the Northeast, with yellow flesh and a sweet flavor; the *Empire,* an upstate New York apple that is crisp and crunchy to bite; and the *Gravensten,* another two-toned apple grown out west. This apple will rank with any as far as flavor is concerned, though it is not much to look at.

Apples are available year round, but the peak season is August through October. Select apples that are bruise-free and firm to the touch. Refrigerate apart from strong-smelling foods. Apples are rich in vitamins A, B, and C, fiber, iron and potassium.

Apricots

Like its relatives nectarines and peaches, apricots are native to China. Cots (a common name for apricots) originated some three to four thousand years ago. The fruit made its way west through Europe and became very popular in the Mediterranean. It's believed that some of the first settlers brought apricots to America; however, they didn't do well on this continent until the 1700s, when Spanish padres planted apricots throughout California as they opened new missions. At one point during the 1970s California produced over 85 percent of the apricots grown in the United States as well as accounting for at least 45 percent of the worldwide output.

This fragile fruit is almost as pleasant to look at as it is to taste. From the reddish-orange skin of the *Katy* variety to the bright orange of the *Tilton,* the apricot is a beautiful fruit.

Apricots reach their peak flavor when allowed to tree ripen, so you probably won't get to taste apricots at their best unless you have an apricot tree in your backyard. When ripe, the apricot is the most fragile of all summer fruits. Therefore very few if any ripe apricots are shipped to wholesale or retail markets.

With that in mind, select firm fruit when shopping, for it will ripen at room temperature in two or three days and achieve a full and pleasant flavor. However, as with other summer fruits, color is the key. If the fruit was harvested before obtaining a full orange or red blush, it is very likely to become sour or shrivel before it softens and ripens.

Not too long ago only a few apricots varieties were sold in retail outlets: *Royal, Derby, Stewart,* and *Blenheim.* The four are so similar in appearance and taste that they are marketed under the same name, Royals. The original Royal was brought over from France in 1850 and was planted in northern California the Winters area, which produces more apricots than any single area in the world. Today there are many varieties making quite an impact on the market, such as the Katy, the *Patterson,* and the improved *Flaming Gold,* just to name a few. The new hybrid varieties are bigger and have strong colors, but their flavors just cannot surpass the Royal varieties. The season for fresh apricots runs May through August, peaking July through August.

Remember, firm apricots will ripen in two or three days on your countertop. Then store them in the refrigerator till you are ready to eat them. The apricot is a good source for vitamin A and contains some vitamin C. For the calorie-conscious, one fresh apricot contains only about twenty calories.

Avocados

I call these my California fruit, because I had never tasted one until I moved out west. However, the picture writing of the Aztec and Mayan civilizations proves that this native American crop was being used as food long before Columbus made his way west. The pictures are as old as 300 B.C., but the avocado did not appear in North America until the nineteenth century. This nonsweet fruit (yes, the avocado is a fruit, although many produce people discuss them as if they were vegetables) was first planted in Florida during the 1830s. That same century Spanish missionaries introduced the avocado to Califorina.

As an industry, avocado farming began around the turn of the twentieth century both in Florida and California. Although both states cultivate fruits called by the same name, the two states produce two totally different types of avocados. The Florida avocado came up from eastern South America and the West Indies. In Florida, as in the islands, the soil is much looser, the rainfall heavier, and the humidity higher than in California. In these conditions, the fruit grows to much larger sizes, but also has a higher water content, resulting in a less nutty flavor than its California counterpart. Some of the popular Florida varieties are **Walden, Booth,** and **Lula,** but in stores they are usually marketed under one name: Florida avocado. The California avocado, thanks to climate, has thicker skin, a richer, thicker texture, and, of course, less watery content. The flavor is quite nutty. Some say eating California avocados is like drinking fresh brewed coffee, whereas Florida avocados are like instant decaf.

Here are some California varieties:

The **Bacon,** which looks very much like a Florida avocado. During the early days of Peaches Produce, I got into a few verbal fights over that large, pitted, watery, smooth-skinned variety. I just refused to pay the wholesaler the California price for what I thought was a Florida avocado. I had to make some apologies when I learned the Bacon was from the West Coast.

The **Zutano** is medium-sized like the Bacon, but with more of a pear shape. It is available in markets from late fall through the winter. In the produce business it's called a winter variety.

The **Fuerte** was the only variety not wiped out during the California freeze of 1913. In Spanish *fuerte* means "strong." The Fuerte is by far the most popular winter avocado. If you're not careful, you could mistake it for a green Bosc pear. This variety, with medium-thick skin and a mild, nutty flavor, is second only to the Hass variety.

I've saved the best for last: the **Hass.** This oval-shaped beauty is in season April through late November. The bumpy, thick green skin darkens as the fruit ripens until it's a shiny jet black. The flavor, unsurpassed anywhere, is very rich, wal-nutty, and quite oily—so oily that out west many people use avocados as a skin conditioner.

Until recently avocados were thought of as exotic or as food for the rich and famous, but now thanks to the California Avocado Commission and increased production, consumers from all walks of life enjoy this richly nutritional fruit. The avocado supplies high amounts of vitamins A, B, and C, and it is loaded with potassium. However, California avocados are also high in fat and calories. With that in mind, you may want to consider the Florida varieties, which have about half the calories and fat—though I should point out that avocado fat in not concentrated, so it is not as unhealthy as palm fat or animal fat.

California avocados have a twelve-month season, whereas Florida has only an eight-month season, so Florida avocados are not available during spring. When shopping remember that as with pears and bananas, avocados never reach their flavorful peak until after being harvested; they do not ripen fully on the tree. This is an advantage because it means you can control the ripening of your own fruit. Always select hard green fruit free of cuts. When you take them home, place them in a brown paper bag and put the bag in a warm spot. (I always put mine on top of my refrigerator.) Check them daily, for they will ripen fast: Florida varieties take three to four days, the Califor-nia four to six days. **To speed the ripening time to about half that, add a tomato to the bag.** The natural gases released by the tomato speed up the process.

There are three ways I especially enjoy avocados: I love them sliced on crackers or sliced with tomatoes and onion (no dressing needed) but my all-time favorite is guacamole. Here is a guacamole recipe I got from Eddie and Mary Ayub in San Diego:

GUACAMOLE

Ingredients:
   3 avocados
   juice from 1 lemon
   1/2 tbs. mayo
   1 med. onion, diced

Instructions:
   Peel and pit avocado, slice into bowl, mash up, mix in lemon juice, mayo, and onion. If you like hot things add ground jalapeno or hot finger pepper. You can also add salsa.

Bananas

The banana originated in southern Asia, where it was being harvested as food long before most other fruits. Columbus introduced the banana plant to the American tropics, where it thrived. In fact, later explorers believed the plant was native to the West.

Believe it or not, bananas are the world's most popular . . . *berry!* Something else you won't believe is that they don't grow on trees; rather, they grow on giant tropical herbs that look like trees. The botanical name of the berry borne by this giant herb is *musa sapientum,* which means "fruit of the wise men." To us they are more commonly known as bananas, the third most popular fruit in America, ranking just behind apples and oranges.

Most folks say a banana is a banana, and that's pretty much true, but there are two types sold in the United States: the **Cavendish,** which has a flat, blunt end, and the **Gros Michel,** which has a kind of pointed end. This is the only way to tell the two apart; their taste is the same. However, there are some new bananas on the scene that you should put on your buy-and-try list: first, red bananas (red Spanish or red Cuban), and second, little finger bananas, also known as apple bananas. When I worked at Balducci's in New York City, one of our best accounts was the United Nations dining facilities, which of course catered to many international diplomats, one of whom was former Secretary of State George Schultz. Mr. Schultz loves bananas, and I'm told his favorite is the little finger banana, so whenever Mr. Schultz was in New York the UN chef would call up and say, "Curtis the Secretary's coming," and I knew it was time to round up the little finger bananas.

Being a tropical fruit, bananas are available year round and normally sell at reasonable prices. When shopping, choose fruits with an even yellow color. They are perfect for eating and will keep two or three days at room temperature. You can store bananas in the refrigerator, but only after they are ripened; the skin will darken but the flesh will still taste great.

As for nutrition, bananas are loaded with vitamin A, and contain some vitamins B and C. Low in fat, they are a good source for calcium, iron, and phosphorus, and of course, they're an excellent source for potassium, containing 260 milligrams of calcium per banana—and only eighty-eight calories.

Carambola

The *Star fruit*—this exotic and beautiful fruit has an appearance that is totally unique. Native to Malaysia, it now grows very well in Hawaii and the islands of the Carribbean. You can find some star fruit from Florida and California, but remember, the best come from the tropical regions because the trees are very sensitive to cold nights. The flavor of the star fruit ranges from tart and sweet to very sour, depending on variety and ripeness. Your produce person should be able to tell you the name of the variety that is carried in that shop. The sweetest variety is the *Gold Star* when fully ripe. Unripe carambola are pale yellow, have very little flavor, and are very sour. As the fruit ripens, the color changes to a rich dark yellow and the flavor becomes much sweeter.

The season for carambola is September through January, and remember: the key to selecting this exotic fruit is color, which should be dark and yellow, and be sure to ask your produce person for the Gold Star variety. Most star fruits are eaten raw, or in a fruit salad; they may also be chilled inside gelatin, and although I have never tried it this way, I was told by a food stylist in Los Angeles that star fruit is very tasty when sautéed in rosé wine.

The carambola is extremely high in vitamin A and quite low in calories and fat.

Cherimoya

I once received a letter that said , "While traveling in South America I ate this strange fruit that looked like a dark artichoke, with black seeds inside. My traveling companion called it custard fruit." Do you know what it is?

The fruit that the curious traveler wrote about is not strange to South America; in fact, it is native to the cool regions of the Andes Mountains of Peru and Bolivia. It is the cherimoya.

The cherimoya is something special. Although I have never heard it referred to as custard fruit, I have heard it called *custard apple.* The flavor is the special part of this exotic fruit, a mixture of banana, pineapple, and some say, pear. The texture does remind me of custard pie.

The description from the letter is perfect for the ripened fruit; however, since the cherimoya is extremely delicate when ripe, probably few shoppers have seen them in that condition.

When shopping for cherimoya, you should look for a light-green, pear-shaped fruit which at first glance makes you think there is something wrong with this artichoke. The best thing is to ask your produce person for cherimoya. Although cheri-moya is being grown in Californa on a fairly large scale, it is still considered quite exotic and is also very expensive in the United States, so you probably won't find them at your local supermarket unless enough shopper demand them.

The season begins in November and ends in April. Fresh cherimoya makes an excellent addition to any fruit salad, and it will give your guests something to talk about. Eating cherimoya out of hand can be quite trying because of the large, inedible black seeds. I suggest cutting the fruit into quarters, removing the seeds with a knife or fork, then scooping out the flesh with a spoon to eat on the spot or to add to salad.

A medium cherimoya contains about ninety calories, like an apple. It is also a good source of vitamins A and C as well as iron and phosporus. Well-rounded I'd say.

Coconuts

The coconut has been cultivated for so long in the tropical regions of the world that no one has an exact fix on its birthplace. Like its cousin, the date, the coconut is produced on palm trees and just as the date palm is highly regarded in the desert regions of the world, the coconut palm is equally prized in the tropics, not just for the food it produces, but also for its byproducts. Some byproducts of the coconut palm are soaps, margarines, ropes, mats, and many other items, but for me the prize is the milky white flesh of the coconut itself. I love to enjoy fresh coconut as a snack by itself, and it is also great grated over fruit salads. Fresh coconut comes to United States markets from many areas, including the Dominican Republic and Puerto Rico. They are available year round but are most abundant during the fall and winter.

When selecting fresh coconut simply pick it up and shake it up. If you hear a sloshing sound, you have a winner. If not, the coconut is dried out and the flesh may be dry and no good as well.

There must be seven or eight techniques for opening a coconut, but all of them involve poking out one or two of the dark brown spots located at the top of the nut, called eyes. After poking out the eyes, drain the liquid, which may be chilled and enjoyed as a drink or added to other liquid refreshment to enhance taste. Then place the nut on a hard surface and hit it squarely between the eyes with a hammer or, as the early Hawaiians did, with a big rock; a split should occur right down the middle. Then simply pry open your coconut and pull the flesh away from the shell. Two other methods of opening a coconut are first, you may freeze it, which makes the hard shell much more brittle, so that it cracks easily when struck by a hammer; or you may place the drained coconut in a pre-heated 400-degree oven for fifteen to twenty minutes until it cracks open.

Coconuts will keep for months as long as you don't poke out the eyes. Like most of the other hard fruits (nuts), coconuts are also quite high in calories. However, this body-building fruit is a good source for protein, iron, and phosphorus.

Dates

Fresh dates can be traced back to about 3500 B.C. In the Middle East, where dates were first cultivated, every part of the fruit was used. Date cakes were made from the meat, honey from the juice, and oil from the seed. Not only was the fruit a great prize because of its many uses, but the palm tree on which it grew was equally valuable. The center of the date palm could be pounded into flour, and from the sap a rather potent alcoholic beverage was brewed. The leaves were used in many ways, and the fiber was made into very strong rope.

Dates were introduced to North America by the Spanish missionaries along the California and Mexican coast lines; however, the date palm did not thrive on this continent until the early part of this century, when Dr. W. T. Swingle brought an Algerian variety (*Deglet Noor,* which means "date of the night") to the deserts of southern California, where the city of Indio stands today, in the Coachella Valley.

Over one hundred varieties are grown in California alone, but of all those varieties one accounts for 95 percent of the total annual date sales in the United States. This is the same variety Dr. Swingle introduced some eighty years ago, the Deglet Noor.

The Deglet Noor is a semi-dry date. When ripe it is amber in color and very tasty. You may want to try others, but be aware that they are hard to find. Two of these are the *Medjool,* a rather large, attractive sweet date, and the *Barhi,* the softest and most delicate of the dates.

Fresh dates make an excellent snack out of hand and are also nice to bake with. Mix in some chopped fresh dates the next time you make banana bread, or when a recipe calls for nuts, substitute dates. They are also good to mix when making homemade candies.

Fresh dates are available starting in May, with the season winding down in September. When shopping, choose dates that are high in color and moist and soft to the touch. Remember, dry fruit is old fruit The fruit will keep for weeks wrapped in plastic in the refrigerator.

Dates are very nourishing, being loaded with potassium, calcium, iron, and phosphorus. However, like nuts, they are high in calories.

Figs

This is one of the oldest fruits known to man, if not the oldest. The fig originated in Asia, and as humankind grew and branched out from the Garden of Eden, so too did this ancient fruit. Turkey, Greece, and Italy all became home to this wonderful food item. To this day, figs remain a major crop in all those countries. However, it was the Spanish who introduced the fig to America and some of the world's best and most flavorful are now grown in California.

It's a shame that most of the figs sold retail in the United States are dried because those who have tried fresh figs know how sweet and juicy and refreshing they are. There are many varieties of figs, but only two basic types: light (green and/or white) and dark (black or deep purple). I think the dark varieties offer the best flavor. If you're not a fresh fig eater, it's time to become one.

For first-timers I recommend the *Mission fig,* sometimes called the *Black Mission.* The skin color is so deep purple it looks black, and the flesh is pink and oh, so sweet. The Mission is my favorite and it's also the leading commercial type. After you fall in love with the Mission, try the *Brown Turkey Fig,* another of the dark varieties, with soft red flesh that is rich in flavor.

Calimyrnas is a large fig three to four inches in diameter, and *Kodoka* is a violet-fleshed fig; both are excellent light varieties to start with. Both have a nice, sweet flavor and are quite juicy.

When shopping for fresh figs, choose fruits soft to the touch and dark in color—deep purple or black in the dark varieties and golden yellow in the light ones. Color and softness are good signs of peak flavor and ripeness. Fresh figs are available June through November, with the season peaking in September and October.

As for nutrition, figs are good energy food, so instead of a candy bar, try a fresh fig. They are an excellent source of sugar but are low in calories, containing about only fifty per large fig. For other ways to enjoy fresh figs, keep in mind that figs and vanilla ice cream makes a wonderful dessert. However, my favorite way to enjoy a fresh fig is to slice it and eat it by itself.

Grapefruit

As recently as eighty years ago, the grapefruit was all but unknown outside Florida. The parent of today's grapefruit is called *pomelo;* like the other members of the citrus family, it originated in Asia. The pomelo was about twice the size of a large modern grapefruit, had thick puffy skin, and was very sour and filled with seeds. During the late seventeenth century a sailor named Shaddock transplanted some pomelo seeds to the West Indies (later pomelos were also known as Shaddocks), and around the same time a former officer in the French navy planted pomelo seeds in Florida, laying the foundation for the world's best and largest production area for the grapefruit.

By the time the pomelo, a sour citrus, was introduced to the New World, the mandarin orange, a sweet citrus, had been introduced a hundred years earlier and had become well established. Within forty years of the pomelo's introduction to the same tropical regions, cross-pollination took place between the sweet and sour citrus, yielding a new, unnamed fruit. Too sour to be an orange, yet too sweet to be a pomelo, at first this new fruit was small and grew in clusters like grapes on a vine. That's where the name "grapefruit" came from.

It's funny that this once unnamed fruit is now being grown the world over. Producing countries include Greece, Spain, Cuba, Brazil, and Israel. However, none of those countries can match the output and quality of homegrown grapefruits. The United States leads in production, with Florida being the main producer, followed by Texas, California, and Arizona. As for which are the best-tasting, the Texas growers claim that none are as sweet and juicy as their beautiful, sunset-tinted, pink-or-red-fleshed grapefruits, the first citrus to be patented. Texas grapefruits are marketed under several names: **Pink Marsh, Thompson, Ruby,** and **Ruby Red.** They are all something special.

On the other hand, there is Florida, without which there would be no grapefruit industry. As I said, during the early part of this century the only people to taste grapefruit were those who had visited Florida. When sunshine growers finally began shipping their new fruit to regions outside Florida, they were pleasantly surprised with sales figures. Today the Sunshine State not only leads in United States production and sales, with Florida grapefruits accounting for nearly eighty percent of America's annual crop, but the state also leads in world production: Florida grapefruits account for well over half the worldwide output of the fruit. Florida grapefruit can be found in the Orient, in Europe, and just about anywhere there is a taste for citrus. Giving fuel to the Florida growers' case that they have the best grapefruit is the state's crown jewel, the **Marsh White,** one of the world's best grapefruits, if not *the* best. In fact, it's the only commercially grown light-fleshed grapefruit. The skin is a nice, smooth yellow with medium thickness, making it easy to peel (also true of the **Texas Ruby**) and it's juicy and nearly seedless.

Texas and Florida both have famous growing areas. In the Lone Star State it's the Rio Grande Valley near Mexico. Florida's pride is the Indian River Region; between Daytona in the north and Palm Beach in the south, this area is perfect for citrus growing. Now, within Indian River is an area named Orchid Island, and every piece of fruit shipped from that area bears a label saying Orchid or Orchid Island. This is the sign of the world's best, and the price tag matches the quality. Remember, the Gulf Stream is out in the Atlantic, so warm temperatures protect the groves at night when the mildest frost could wipe out an entire industry. (Maybe I shouldn't talk about frost; the Texas crop was destroyed during the early part of the 1980s by such a demon and is just getting back on track in the past few years).

When shopping for grapefruit, choose heavy fruit of uniform size. Don't bother about rough skin or skin color, for it's the weight that tells you whether it's nice and juicy. Grapefruit are available year round, with Florida producing them September through July; Texas, October through July; California, October through February; and Arizona, October through summer. The grapefruit is not quite as nutritious as the other citrus fruits, but it does contain small amounts of vitamins A and B and fair amounts of vitamin C and is low in calories.

Grapes

The grape was introduced to California by Spanish padres as they opened missions throughout the west. However, by no means was this the first introduction of the fruit to America. In fact, hundreds of years before Columbus found America, the Viking sailors crossed the Great North Sea and visited what is now the New England coastline. They were amazed to see the abundance of native grapevines, so they called the area "Vinland."

The grape is believed to be the first fruit cultivated by humans. Its association with man is well-documented throughout the Bible. According to the book of Genesis, one of the first things that Noah did after the Flood was to plant a vineyard. The grape has been around so long and seems to be native to so many lands that its exact origin remains unknown.

There are literally hundreds of varieties of this ancient fruit: two Native American grapes are the **Northern Fox** and the **Muscadine** (this one is still enjoyed in the southern United States). These are considered the parents of today's commercially grown native grapes: the **Niagara,** the **Delaware,** and the most popular of the domestic grapes, the **Concord.** These varieties for the most part are used for eating out of hand. They have thick skins and seeds.

The vineyards planted by the padres are direct descendents of the Old World grapes described in the Bible. They have thinner skins and an overall sweeter flavor. Some of today's table grapes include the **Perlette,** a small green seedless grape with a somewhat thick skin. It grows in a tight cluster and has a nice sweet flavor.

Today's most popular grape is the **Thompson Seedless**— this large, green grape sometimes is as long as one inch. When you see this seedless grape with a rich yellow color, that indicates the sugar levels are at their highest.

Another grape is the **Flame Seedless**—many think this red seedless will surpass the Thompson in popularity, but I don't think so. It has beautiful color and a wonderful sweet flavor, but it's just not as juicy as the Thompson.

If any grape can become more popular than the Thompson, I think it will be the **Exotic.** The Exotic is a black seedless grape that is just a little smaller than the Thompson, but is just as sweet and juicy. As soon as farmers catch on, watch out Thompson! This grape adds beauty to any fruit arrangement.

The forerunner to the Exotic is the **Ribier.** This black grape is surpassed by none as far as flavor, but today most consumers want seedless grapes, and the Ribier has three large pits.

There are many other grapes you should also try. For instance, the **Queen** is a red grape that is sweet, firm, and crisp to bite. The **Tokay** is sure to be a hit in the Nineties—it's the red counterpart to the Perlette. The **Italia** is large, sweet, and juicy with a muscat flavor. Another grape which should become quite popular in the next few years is the **Black Corinth,** more commonly known as the "Champagne Grape," because of its tiny size, like the bubble of its namesake. The flavor is outstanding.

Grapes are available year round. Domestic crops start in late May and wind down in January. During the off-months, the bulk comes in from Chile, and also Mexico, on a smaller level. When shopping for grapes, freshness is key; the fruit should cling firmly to the stem. It should not shake loose easily. The stem should be green with no drying present, which is a sign of age. The fruit will keep up to a week in your refrigerator, but should be consumed within three days if possible.

Grapes aren't known for their nutritional value, but they do contain some vitamins A and C.

Guavas

Those who have tried the guavas grown in Hawaii say that none grown anywhere else on earth can compare. However, the Hawaiian guavas aren't sold on the mainland, and I'm sure you would like to know the reason why this tropical gift can't be found in your local market. Our youngest state happens to be one of the most popular breeding grounds for the fruit fly, and unfortunately, the attractive guava is an ideal host to that dreadful pest. Therefore, this exotic fruit cannot be exported to the mainland unless it has been fumigated. Due to the fragility of the tree-ripened Hawaiian guava, unlike other Hawaiian fruits it cannot withstand the fumigation process; therefore we consumers miss the opportunity to have this fruit on a regular basis.

The origin of the guava is not exactly clear. Some believe it originated in Mexico, but other sources say the Caribbean. However, the guava you are most likely to come across in your local market comes from South Florida. The fruit is light green or yellow in color and about the size of a golfball. The tree-ripened ones I have tried were wonderful, even though they weren't from Hawaii. The flavor is sweet, almost strawberry-like, and the smell is like that of a beautiful flower. The seeds are edible also.

When shopping choose firm, bruise-free guavas that have a slight give at the blossom end. The ripe fruit has one of the most pleasant smells given by nature. Firm guavas will store unrefrigerated for two or three days; after the fruit has softened it should be refrigerated until you are ready to consume it.

Like most tropical fruit, the guava is high in vitamin C and relatively low in calories. Put guavas on your list of must-try fruits. The season begins in middle to late July and winds down in October.

Kiwi-fruit

The kiwi originated in China, where it was known as Yang Tao, and made its way to New Zealand during the early part of the twentieth century. In it's home the fruit thrived and was called *Chinese Gooseberry*. In 1960, when New Zealand businessmen thought of marketing this exotic fruit to United States consumers, they knew a product called *Gooseberry* would be a hard sell. So another name change was in store for the ancient Yang Tao. From then on, the fruit has been called kiwi fruit, a name taken from the bird native to New Zealand. The bird is little, brown, and fuzzy, just like the fruit. Those New Zealanders did such a good job marketing the kiwi fruit that most people think is native to New Zealand.

During the 1960s the kiwi crop was introduced to southern California and has since become a major cash crop. Shoppers are lucky, with New Zealand being in the southern hemisphere, and California in the northern hemisphere, they have reverse growing seasons, so kiwi is available year round. California kiwi is in season November through late May. New Zealand, May through December.

As for taste, I don't think I can do the kiwi justice, but it's fantastic—sweet and tangy. The flesh color is lime green with hundreds of tiny, edible black seeds.

When you bite into a kiwi, you might think it it is loaded with calories. WRONG! The average size kiwi contains only about thirty calories and that same piece of fruit provides over half the daily requirement of vitamin C.

Kiwi is also wonderful to cook with; it is one of those fruits that are natural meat tenderizers as is papaya. Take peeled kiwi and rub it into beef steak before cooking your favorite way. Also, I love to marinate chicken in kiwi, white wine, and a bit of salt and pepper. The chicken is great grilled or baked. Another way to enjoy this Asian delight is with cream. And kiwi juice added to iced tea makes a refreshing drink But my favorite way to eat kiwi fruit remains just to peel them and eat them.

When shopping, choose firm unbruised fruit and allow to ripen at room temperature two to three days. When the fruit is ripe it will keep four to five additional days in the refrigerator.

A special note: The kiwi fruit, since being introduced to America in the early Sixties, is the only fruit to decrease in price while it has increased in demand.

Melons

My all-time favorite melon is, to the best of my knowledge, grown only in California. It is the result of cross-pollinating at least three melons and it's called the *Crane melon.* The skin is smooth and cream-colored, like that of honeydew melon. When ripe, the color changes to a light orange, the melon smells tropically sweet, and the inside reveals a deep sunset orange color and has a flavor that is tangy sweet.

Another nice choice is the *Cranshaw,* the third highest selling melon in America. This melon has yellow skin and gold flesh. When ripe, it is, bar none, the sweetest and juiciest of all melons. I think the Cranshaw tastes best when ice-cold. Its season runs August through December. Remember, if you like it sweet, the Cranshaw is your melon.

The next melon I suggest is the *Persian,* but it has a very short season—August to early October. When ripe it looks like a super-sized cantaloupe. Never buy Persian melons that are green in color; they are not ripe and will never reach their peak flavor. When you pick a Persian with that light orange color, you are in for a special treat.

Now, if you really need a change, ask your produce person for a *Sharlyn melon,* though it might be hard to get because it's fairly new. The Sharlyn has white flesh, which makes it stand out in fruit salads—and its flavor allows it to stand alone. It's sweet like the Cranshaw, but not as juicy.

If it's winter,and you want a melon grown in America, what do you do? Ask for the *Santa Claus.* Where did that name come from, you ask? Before we imported melons from Europe and South America, it was the only melon available at Christmas, so we named it Santa Claus. It looks like a big green football with stripes—long on looks, but short on flavor.

If you want fresh and sweet during winter, I recommend the *Galia melon.* The best are jet-flown from Israel, which makes them a bit costly, but to have a sweet and juicy melon like this for Christmas, we have to pay a little more. In recent years growers in Latin America and Puerto Rico have begun to ship the Galia to the United States. They taste pretty good, but remember—the best are from Israel.

Now that you have six recommendations, I bet you'd like to know how to pick ripe melons. Most experts say there are three keys: sight, touch, and smell. I think there is a fourth: buying melons that are in season. Cantaloupe and honeydew are available year round, peaking June through November; Honeyloupe, August through November; Cranshaw, Persian, and Sharlyn, August through October; and Santa Claus, November through February. Keep in mind that most melons peak around midseason. Choose even-colored melons and make sure there is no mold showing—this is the sight factor. As for touch, choose melons that are firm around the middle with a little give at the blossom end. Regarding smell, immature melons have little or no odor, but when ripe they are as fragrant as a flowerbed.

Uncut melons will keep three to four days unrefrigerated and up to a week refrigerated. After being cut, they should be consumed within two days. As a group, melons are a good source for vitamins A and C. They are also a good source for protein, yet remain low in calories, which is hard to believe since melons are considered some of nature's sweetest gifts.

Pepinos

The pepino is one of the most exciting newcomers to the world of exotic and fancy fruits. The pepino is a melon, although to look at it you would never guess. It is shaped like a miniature football, three to six inches long. The skin is purple with yellowish stripes. The flesh is the part of this South American native that reveals its melon secret. With its pretty, yellow-orange color, the texture and flavor reminds me of a ripe cantaloupe or honeydew. Its color is a yellowish-orange which is quite pleasing to the eye and makes a wonderful addition to fruit salad. The pepino is high in potassium as well as vitamin C. Although most pepino sold in America comes from New Zealand, California has begun to produce the fruit as a cash crop.

The pepino is available starting late January, running through mid-summer. As for selecting the pepino, most fruit sold in retail stores in the United States is still quite green, so be sure to choose fruit without scars or bruises and allow to ripen at room temperature, or until flesh shows that yellow tint and the outer skin is softer.

Watermelons

It is hard to believe that the watermelon is a member of the same botanical family as squash and cucumbers, but it is. This edible gourd originated in Africa. The early African tribesmen would carry watermelons on long hunting trips as a source of moisture, when fresh water would be hard to come by. This melon was brought to America by the early European settlers and, as it did in its homeland of Africa and on the contintent of Europe, watermelon rather quickly became a favorite throughout the thirteen colonies. Watermelons are now grown in more than half of the continental United States. California leads the way in production; however, the southern states lead the way when it comes to taste, and heading up that group is my home state of Georgia, which I believe produces the sweetest, most juicy watermelons in the country.

There are many watermelon varieties, and they come in all shapes, sizes, and colors. The flesh color can be red or yellow, and over the past few years I have been seeing orange flesh. I should point out that the latter two can be and often are many times just as sweet as the red-flesh watermelon. However, red watermelon outsells yellow and orange at least eight to one.

Here are some of the more popular varieties: Out West, the solid green **Peacock** has been a long-time favorite, but one of the southern favorites, the oval-shaped pale green **Charleston Gray,** is quickly gaining popularity. Here in the South and on the East Coast, along with the Charleston Gray, other excellent watermelons include the **Crimson Sweet,** another pale green melon; and the Jubilee, a light green variety with dark green stripes (this one has a flesh color that is fire-engine red and is very sweet). My favorite is the **Black Diamond;** the best of these come from Franklin County, Georgia. The Diamond comes round or somewhat oval with a skin color so dark green that it looks black. Inside, the rind is snow-white and the meat is a beautiful red, not as rich in color as the Jubilee, but equally pretty and oh, so sweet.

In Canada, the *icebox melons* are preferred. This is the smaller variety of watermelon, weighing from two to ten pounds. Leading that pack is the little sweet **Sugar Baby** melon, a miniature version of the Black Diamond.

Watermelons are available year round, but if you are like me and prefer the domestic varieties, you'll find them on the market from late April through November. At other times of year, they come up from Mexico and Central America.

How to select a good watermelon? Most of us who have been in this business a little while try to side-step the question because it is hit-and-miss when it comes to picking a good watermelon. You can thump and slap as much as you want and still pick a bad watermelon. When the real pros, the growers, think a field is ripe and ready to be picked, they cut ten to fifteen melons just to see if the taste and color are ready. So the only way to really tell if you have picked a good melon is after you have cut it and tried it.

As for nutrition, watermelons are quite low in calories, and are an excellent source for potassium. They also provide a fair amount of vitamin A and calcium.

Nectarines

Nectarines, like their distant cousin, peaches, originated centuries ago in China and made their way west along ancient trade routes. One country along that route was Greece, where the fruit was so popular its juice was called the "drink of the gods." The Greek word for that is nektar, thus the name nectarine. Here in the United States, nectarines have always been popular in the areas where they are grown, but until 1940 the fruit had one major drawback. When ripe, it was very soft and delicate. It could not withstand the torture of shipment, so nectarines remained a very localized fruit, until the development of the first gold flesh freestone (the flesh does not adhere to the seed) variety in La Grande, California, about ninety years after the first freestone peach was developed. Like that first peach, the Elberta, the first nectarine, **La Grande,** is still in production.

Since the development of the La Grande, a hybrid nectarine which is able to withstand the punishment of shipment, the nectarine has enjoyed increasing popularity throughout America and the world. Since 1940 over one hundred new varieties of nectarines have been introduced; however, out of all the different nectarines grown in the United States, twelve make up the bulk of the fruit sold to retail consumers: *May Grand, Early Sun Grand, Fire Bright, Spring Red, Red Diamond, Flavor Top, Summer Grand, Fiesta, Royal Giant, Red Gem, Flame-Kist,* and *Red Gold.*

Selecting nectarines is pretty much like selecting peaches. Choose hard fruit, for they will ripen at room temperature, and avoid fruit that still shows green in the color of the skin. Like peaches, nectarines are an excellent source for Vitamin A; however, they are a bit higher in calories. The seasons run pretty much the same as for peaches: June through September.

Oranges

The best oranges are grown in the west, although *Jaffa* (the name the Israeli navel orange is marketed under) oranges from Israel are quite good. There are many varieties; however, two stand out for me. My favorite, *Valencia* (best for fresh orange juice) is the pineapple orange. This little, round, beautiful orange is sweet and juicy; it has a lot of seeds, but that's OK if you like good taste. The name comes from the sweet smell.

The best orange for eating out of hand is the *navel.* The Florida navels are big, sweet, and very juicy. The peels aren't quite as thick as their West Coast counterpart, due to Florida's hot days and warm nights, which sometimes keep the peel from becoming completely orange. It's OK to buy Florida oranges that show green in the peel. They will still be sweet and juicy. The California navel has a thick skin which makes it very easy to peel, and the segments much easier to divide. The orange color of the West Coast navel is very deep when compared to Florida's crop and they're not as juicy, but are just as sweet. My favorite navel orange is the Washington Navel. No, they are not grown in Washington State. This orange came to America by way of Brazil. Missionaries sent the Department of Agriculture several trees in the mid-1800s. The offspring of those trees still thrive today in California.

Remember, oranges are available year round but the most volume and best quality can be found from November through

April and some into May. Don't concern yourself with the color, as much as the weight of the orange, and make sure the skin has not dried out. And oranges are loaded with vitamin C.

Papaya

Even though it's an American native, the papaya was considered strange and exotic here until the mid-twentieth century. This pear-shaped delight is believed to have originated in Central or South America. It rapidly spread throughout the tropical region of this hemisphere.

The first time I saw papaya dangling from a tree was in the summer of '88 in Key West, Florida. I was visiting the historical site that was once the home of Ernest Hemingway. To the left of the main house is a garden cut out of the coral reef on which Key West sits. In that garden was a papaw tree that stood twenty feet tall; dark green in color from stalk to the tip of its leaves, it was an absolutely beautiful plan. The fruit the pawpaw tree bears is the papaya, and this one was dangling from what looked like long green ropes. I had to restrain myself from plucking that papaya from Papa Hemingway's tree.

In the American tropics, many varieties still grow in the wild. Some are less than two inches long and weigh just ounces; others grow to be as large as volleyballs, weighing pounds. It wasn't until the 1800s that the papaya was introduced to its ideal tropical region, Hawaii, which by far is the largest supplier of fresh papaya to the mainland United States.

The variety most often cultivated in Hawaii is the *Solo*. Unlike the wild varieties, the Solo grows more uniformly, is six to eight inches long, and weighs about one to two pounds, which makes it perfect for packing and shipping. The Solo is a beautiful yellow variety that is extremely sweet and juicy.

There is another variety grown in Hawaii that unfortunately is not available to the mainland consumer. It is the *Sunrise,* which is even sweeter than the Solo, and has more of a reddish-orange color. I think the American consumer would absolutely love the Sunrise papaya. However, like other delicate tropical fruits, the Sunrise papaya can't withstand the fumigation process required before shipment to the mainland.

The papaya is truly one of nature's wonderful gifts. In addition to its exquisite flavor, it is a natural meat tenderizer, which makes it excellent for cooking.

Selecting papaya is simple. The fruit ripens from bottom to top, or blossom end to stem. Its color changes from green to sunshine yellow, much like a banana, and as its color changes, the sugar content rises. I have found that when about one-fourth of the papaya has turned yellow, its sugar content is high enough for the fruit to be quite tasty. Also, at that point it is perfect to cook with.

After the papaya has fully ripened, it can be stored in the refrigerator two or three days.

There are very few fruits that are as naturally sweet as the papaya, yet remain as low in calories (about thirty-nine per serving). It is an excellent source for vitamins A, B, and C, and also contains large amounts of phosphorus and potassium. Here are the two good papaya recipes:

First, a papaya sauce that is excellent over vegetables or meat dishes.

PAPAYA SAUCE

Ingredients:
>   1/2 papaya
>   dash of salt and pepper
>   1 tsp. lemon juice

Instructions:
>   In saucepan, combine all ingredients. Bring to a simmer. Pour into blender. Puree. Return mixture to saucepan. Simmer again. Serve over chicken or vegetables.

Papaya Roasted Chicken

Ingredients:
> 1 chicken, cut up
> 1 papaya, seeded and diced
> 1/2 green pepper
> 1/2 onion, diced
> Salt and pepper to taste

Instructions:
> In roasting pan, place one layer of diced papaya. Place chicken on top of papaya. Smother with remaining ingredients. Roast in preheated 325 degree oven 20 to 30 minutes (longer if needed).

Passion Fruit

Like the cherimoya, the Passion Fruit is native to South America. The fruits have other similarities as well. Both thrive in subtropical and tropical regions of the world. When they are ripe, they have very unusual appearances.

The common name, Passion Fruit, does not come from the fruit's ability to stimulate romantic endeavors, although most retailers would lead you to believe that. The truth is quite the opposite.

Until quite recently, the *granadilla* or Passion Plant was cultivated for its ornamental value—to be more specific, its flower. The early Christian missionaries to South America are believed to have renamed this flower "Passion Flower" after observing similarities between the flower's inner petals and the crown of thorns placed on the head of Jesus Christ, and other symbols of the crucifixion. So the name is really in honor of the passion of Christ.

My first encounter with Passion Fruit came during my second week at Peaches Produce in San Francisco. A customer ordered a case, and I was so disappointed when I delivered this box of wrinkled-looking fruit that had some mold on it. I promised my customer that the next case would be perfect; he looked at me and laughed long and hard. He finally said, "Curtis, these *are* perfect. That's what the fruit looks like when it is ripe."

The taste is very exotic (sweet, with a little tartness) and the smell is truly heavenly. The season runs March through September. To select, choose fruit high in color, in the New Zealand variety, purple; Hawaiian, a little lighter in color. If the shell is smooth and hard, allow the fruit time to ripen at room temperature. You will know it is ready to eat when the fruit has wrinkled and shriveled and the shell has become much softer.

As for nutrition, although Passion Fruit is quite sweet and provides some vitamin C, it remains very low in calories—about fifteen per fruit.

Peaches

Many areas of the world are proud producers of this ancient fruit. during winter, Chile and Australia are among the countries that ship fresh peaches to the United States, and at home, states fight to lay claim to various peach honors. Arizona and California bicker each year about which state will produce the first peach of the domestic season. New Jersey and Pennsylvania argue over which state produces the best peach north of the Mason-Dixon Line. In the South, South Carolina lays claim to number one as far as peach production, but no state dare claim it produces a better peach than Georgia.

How did the Chinese symbol of long life become a proud product of American agriculture? In 1850, the Rumphy family of Georgia received peach buddings from China. The trees grew and produced like crazy. Supposedly, Mrs. Rumphy dropped several pits into a basket and forgot about them until years later, when her grandson started his orchard. He planted the pits and this cling-type peach (the flesh adheres to the seed) tree grew and bloomed. Cross pollination took place between the new trees and older ones. The end result of that fluke of nature was a golden freestone (seed is loose inside the fruit) variety which young Rumphy named Elberta, after his wife. The Elberta is worlds apart from the small, hard, and sour peach that originated in China centuries before the birth of Christ.

The *Elberta* peach—son of the cling variety, and considered father to all the freestone peaches, was once so popular that it alone accounted for over 90 percent of the total peach sales in the United States annually. Today, that percentage has dropped to about 50 percent. If you are still not clear about cling and freestone peaches maybe this will help. If you took a cling peach, and sliced it in half, flesh would adhere to the seed. Do the same process to a freestone, and the seed would pop right out.

As popular as the Elberta was, and still is, there are many other great tasting peaches you may want to look for and try. Here are a few: white peaches, the early *Babcok,* and a Southern favorite, *Georgia Belle.* As for the yellow and red flesh, try the Ladies: *June Lady* and *Elegant Lady.* Both have attractive red skin and beautiful golden flesh with tints of red. Other national favorites are *O-Henry, Red Haven,* and the *Fay Elberta.*

When selecting fresh peaches, it is fine to choose hard fruit, because it will ripen at room temperature, and they are good for cooking. However, avoid peaches that still show green in the color of the skin. Those peaches were harvested too soon and most times dry out before ripening completely. Now, the key to choosing sweet and juicy peaches is at the end of your face. Don't be afraid to follow your nose. If it smells peachy, then it tastes peachy. The season begins in May and peaks in mid-June through August. The entire season winds down in September. You can find domestic peaches available in October, but I recommend avoiding them because they have been in storage for quite some time.

The peach is a great source for vitamin A and is relatively low in calories—a medium peach usually contains about fifty.

Pears

The pear is a member of the rose family like the apple and quince. There are hundreds of varieties of pears in existence, but only a dozen or so are grown commercially.

My favorite pear is a perfect example of the saying that beauty is only skin deep. The *Comice* is ugly, but beneath that peel is the most flavorable, sweet, and juicy pear in the world. In Europe, this pear is such a prize that shoppers anticipate its arrival one month before the season begins, and in the some restaurants it is served as a dessert alone. Its season is October through November, but is still available from storage through the winter. The next pear, if it were entered in a beauty contest, would take first prize hands down. The *Bosc* is the most shapely of pears—when ripe it has a dark tan color. This pear is not very juicy, but is quite sweet and has a nutty flavor. I think the Bosc is best when still very firm and crunchy. They're available October through May.

The next two pears are used primarily as decorations. The *Forelle,* most experts say, is long on looks and short on flavor, but I think they are very wrong. When ripe, this shapely freckled miniature pear is sweet and still crisp when you buy it. Sometimes, though, you will run into a tart Forelle. Don't let that discourage you from buying it; this pear is great on a cheese platter.

Most pears were introduced to this country from Europe and other parts of the world, but the Seckel pear is a North American native. It was discovered in Pennsylvania in the early 1800s near the Delaware River. This is the smallest of all varieties of pears; it is not much larger than a golf ball. When ripe it is dull green with red cheeks. The *Seckel* pear is an eastern pear, but the best are grown out west in California, Oregon, and Washington. This is a sweet and juicy little pear whose season is September through January.

The *Williams Pear,* more commonly known in America as the *Bartlett,* is the world's best-selling pear. It is the first pear of the season starting in late summer and is available fresh well into fall. Over the past few years, the red Bartlett has been gaining in popularity. It's not quite as sweet as its more familiar yellow older brother, but does possess outstanding flavor.

The most popular winter pear is the *Anjou.* It was introduced to America during the mid 1800s. The Anjou looks similar to the Bartlett with a shorter top, and when ripe is not quite as yellow.

Pears are available year round, but with most of the domestic varieties, the season runs late summer through later winter. You should select firm, unscarred fruit, and allow it to ripen at room temperature. You can tell pears are ripe when you press against the stem end and there is a slight give. There is an exception to every rule, and the Bosc pear is the one exception to this rule.

Out of all the deciduous fruits, pears are the highest in calorie count (ninety) and sugar. However, they are also loaded with carbohydrates, calcium, and potassium.

FRUIT & SORBET DELIGHT:

Ingredients:
>   1 Comice pear
>   6 to 8 oz. of assorted berries
>   berry sorbet

Instructions:
>   Slice the large berries and arrange 3/4 of the berries in a bed in a dish for the pear. Peel and core the Comice pear, place the pear on top of the berry bed. Place the remaining sliced berries inside the pear, then pour the berry sorbet over the top.

Persimmons

The persimmon is an autumn fruit, like the pomegranate. When I was growing up, there was a pretty little tree with large berries on it in our backyard. Later I found out they were not berries at all; they were persimmons (not the big shapely varieties you find in gourmet stores today, but the smaller, less attractive ones that are native to North America, the southern states in particular). If you have ever bitten into an unripe persimmon, you know why my childhood memories of it are sour. It is like biting into a very unripe lime. It just locks your mouth up. No matter how much water you drink, it stays dry. Everyone would tell me, "You just have to pick them when they're ripe; they are so sweet and juicy." Well, finally I gave up on trying to pick a ripe persimmon, until a few years ago when shopping in New York City's Hunt's Point Market. An Old Timer was eating a ripe persimmon and seemed to be truly enjoying it. He taught me the secret to selecting and ripening persimmons.

I remember telling him, "I have never met a persimmon I liked or one that liked me. They always made my mouth feel like the Sahara Desert." His reply was, "You just didn't know what you were buying." Then he said, "Pick yourself a nice, pretty piece of fruit and let it sit until it wrinkles up and becomes nice and soft." I jumped in and said, "Yeah, then is it ripe?" "No, wait two more days. Then it's ripe," was his comeback. He was right. When ripe, very few fruits can match up with persimmons as far as sweetness, and they are so soft and juicy.

The wild persimmons that grew in my backyard when I was a child had very little in common with the persimmons you will find in the retail stores of today. This fruit is native to Asia and is still very popular in that part of the world. The persimmon is like no other fruit; however, the persimmon tree is related to the ebony tree. Ebony wood is used in making expensive furniture, and persimmon wood is used in the manufacturing of wood golf club heads. You know some say the growing popularity of golf is the reason the acreage of persimmon trees has dropped in recent decades. I wonder, now that metal woods have been introduced to golf, if more persimmon trees will be allowed to mature and bear fruit.

There are many varieties of persimmons; however, only two varieties are grown and packed for sale in California, which provides all the United States commercial crops. The first is *Hachiya,* which makes up over 80 percent of all persimmons sold in the United States annually. This type is just beautiful to look at. It is shaped like an acorn, but is much larger, about the size of a nectarine, sometimes weighing as much as a pound and a half. The color is orange, bright, and shiny. Warning! Never bite into the Hachiya persimmon until it is fully ripe because it will lock your mouth up. To be sure a persimmon is ripe, allow it to soften until the skin wrinkles and it is soft to touch.

The *Fuyus* is the other commercially grown variety. It's not too big and not very pretty. This variety looks like a dull orange tomato. Fuyus is not as sweet as the Hachiya, but does have one good thing going: it can be eaten while still firm and not dry your mouth out.

The season for persimmons begins in October and runs through January. You can take an unripe persimmon, freeze it, and when it thaws out it will be completely ripe and sweet. As for nutrition, persimmons have a fair amount of vitamin C, and provide about half the daily recommended allowance of vitamin A. Persimmons are relatively low in calories, about seventy-seven per fruit.

Pineapples

The international symbol of welcome and hospitality is the pineapple. It originated in South America and was spread throughout the tropical areas of the world by the early explorers. In Hawaii, during the late 1700s, the pineapple was considered a weed and quite a nuisance. Around 1890 an Englishman, John Kidwell, cultivated the Hawaiian pineapple and set the foundation for the islands' largest industry (until tourism). The three sources that supply the United States market are Central America, Mexico, and Hawaii. Central America sends us the **Red Spanish Pineapple;** this pineapple has a lovely name but that's about all. I don't recommend this pineapple. Mexico ships the **Sugar Loaf;** this is the giant of pineapples, weighing from five to twelve pounds. When you find a ripe sugar loaf, its taste is as good as any other variety. One problem—Mexico has a tendency to ship unripened fruit, and pineapples do not ripen after being picked.

Hawaii grows and ships the best pineapple in the world— the **Smooth Cayenne.** This variety also grows in South Africa and the Philippines, but I doubt that you will find those two areas represented in your local greengrocery. However, during the mid-1980s, the Hawaiian Smooth Cayenne was transplanted with great success to Central America's Costa Rica, among other countries. When ripe, the Hawaiian **Cayenne** is the sweetest, juiciest pineapple in the world. The flavor and sweetness of this transplant to Central America has steadily improved to the point where most of the pineapples sold in the southern United States, and a large part of the East Coast, are shipped from Central America. This is great for consumers because over the past ten years, the pineapple is among the few fruits that has experienced an overall drop in price.

There is one major difference in the Hawaiian and Central American Smooth Cayenne—shell (or skin) color. When ripe, the Hawaiian fruit has a beautiful golden tan shell, whereas the Central American pineapple is green when ripe. However, the growers there have been working to change the color. Personally, I hope they don't succeed; I think it is great to be able to tell the two pineapples apart.

Being a tropical fruit, pineapples are available year round. When shopping, remember shell color is not the most important thing. First, examine the crown (that is the green part that adorns the top of the fruit). It should be green with no dark or dry ends—those are the first signs of age. Next examine the body. Notice the little semi-circle sections of the fruit—they are called eyes. I like to say, "Pineapples are like kids—if you treat them badly, they will cry." Avoid any fruit with leaking eyes or bruises and mold.

The most important key to selecting the perfect-tasting pineapple, be it the golden ripe Hawaiian or the beautiful green Central American, is smell. A ripe pineapple gives off the most wonderful tropical aroma, so don't be afraid to put your nose to work.

Like the kiwi and the papaya, the pineapple contains papain and the pineapple also contains chlorine, which aids in digestion. Those items also make the fruit a natural meat tenderizer; therefore, it is excellent in marinades and cooking with beef, pork, and chicken.

Pineapples provide a wealth of goodness: they are low in calories, high in vitamins A and C, low in fat, rich in calcium, phosphorus, and potassium.

Pomegranates

When I was a child I loved it when my parents would bring home pomegranates; it was like getting candy and a toy at the same time. I had so much fun trying to tear away the rather pretty leathery skin without breaking open the honeycomb-like clusters which held the candy-sweet nectar of the pomegranate. As I got older it didn't seem to be as much fun opening the fruit. I'm sure that is the reason this fruit has not enjoyed the popularity in America that it does in other parts of the world.

Pomegranates are believed to have originated in the Mediterranean region and are still a very popular fruit in that area today. Like apricots, this fruit was planted throughout California by the Spanish padres as they opened new missions on the West Coast. The tree is just beautiful. In summertime its dark green leaves are a wonderful background for the bright orange flowers it produces. And in autumn, when the fruit ripens it's as if God Himself decided to decorate a Christmas tree a few months early.

When selecting pomegranates, choose large fruit that is

heavy for its size, is free from cuts, and has no dark spots. The season begins in September and winds down in December or January. The fruit is rather moderate as far as nutrition is concerned. It contains a trace amount of vitamin A, some vitamin C, about four milligrams, and fair amounts of calcium and phosphorus.

To open a pomegranate, remove the crown (cut it off) with a sharp knife. Make several slices lengthwise down the fruit, being careful not to slice too deep into the pomegranate. Next, place the scored fruit into a bowl of water and soak for five minutes. While holding the fruit in the water, break into sections, separating seeds from membrane with your finger. The seeds will sink to the bottom; the membrane will float to the top. Discard the membrane, rinse and pat dry seeds, then eat.

Quince

The quince originated in Asia, but I doubt that many people are familiar with it, although it is not a new fruit. To the contrary, although the quince is now a forgotten fruit, during the early part of this century it was one of America's most popular produce items.

The quince, like the apple and pear, is a member of the rose family. Its fragrance is like a lovely perfume, and in the days before all the fancy air fresheners, many people kept a display of fresh quince in their homes just for the lovely aroma. As with apple and pear trees, the quince tree flowers in spring and its fruit ripens in fall; however, unlike its relatives, the quince is not good eaten right off the tree or out of hand. When tree-ripened the quince has a pretty, yellow skin, but as a result the flesh is a pale color and extremely tart when eaten raw. No matter how much you enjoy tart fruit, like Granny Smith apples, I doubt you can stand the taste of raw quince.

When cooked, however, especially in a little syrup, the flesh becomes a pinkish color and much of the tartness disappears. Because of all the work people think is necessary to enjoy this fruit, the quince has all but disappeared from retail stores in

America. This is a shame, for preparing quince is not that hard; it's like making an apple pie without a crust. All you do is peel the fruit, core and slice it, season it with nutmeg and cinnamon if you like, add syrup, then simmer about forty-five minutes.

Fresh quince is usually available only during fall, unfortunately, unless you have a tree in the backyard, which is common in the South. The only stores that carry them on a regular basis are the gourmet and specialty shops, so prices tend to be on the upscale.

When shopping for quince, choose firm, unbruised fruit with high yellow color. At home the fruit will keep at least two weeks right on the counter.

The quince is not as nutritious as the apple, but it does contain vitamin A and small amounts of vitamins B and C. It also provides calcium, iron, and phosphorus, and raw it's low in calories, but remember you will be cooking quince in syrup.

Strawberries

The best strawberries I ever ate were grown in Norway. I was in a little town about sixty miles north of Oslo, Hamar, where the 1992 Winter Olympics will be held. Few people would think of Norway as berry country, with its relatively short growing season, but these berries were delicious! Across the street from where I stayed was a farm with a sign which read "All You Can Pick and Carry for 20 Kroner," about four United States dollars. My friend and I picked about four gallons, with many of the berries being as big as tennis balls. The color was a beautiful red, dark but not auburn, and not as light as those wonderful Norwegian sunsets that are just breathtaking. During that visit to the "Land of the Midnight Sun" I fell in love with eating strawberries and cream and have enjoyed that combination ever since.

Strawberries grow wild the world over, and their cultivation dates back hundreds of years. In Europe they were beautiful, but small and not too sweet. The berries native to North America had excellent flavor, but were still small. During the early 1700s European explorers found a rather large variety growing in South America. By cross-breeding the three types, botanists came up with the father of all the hybrid varieties we enjoy today, which include the *Hovey,* the first hybrid strawberry developed in the United States, and the *Wilson,* the *Heidi,* and the *Chander.*

California is by far America's and the world's biggest and best supplier of fresh strawberries. That state is in strawberry production eleven months out of the year, with December being the only down time. During that time Florida picks up the slack, and other berries come in by air shipment from New Zealand. Both those areas produce quite good berries.

Like pineapples, strawberries do not ripen further after being harvested; therefore, selection is very important. When shopping, choose dry, firm berries with rich color that covers the fruit up to the cap (which should always be green—a good sign of freshness). Avoid any berry with a dull or pale color (they are flavorless), and berries that are soft, wet, or showing mold. If stored in brown paper bags in the fruit keeper of your refrigerator, strawberries can keep a week. However, to enjoy the best flavor and receive the most nutrition, they should be consumed within three days.

The strawberry is an excellent skin-cleaning food, and it helps rid the body of harmful toxins. Fresh strawberries are high in vitamins A, B, and C, as well as containing large amounts of potassium and calcium (for their size, of course).

Tangerines, tangelos

My favorite citrus fruits are in the mandarin family, which includes the tangerine, tangelo, and mandarin orange. In your local produce store you will very rarely see a display of mandarin oranges. With this in mind, let's concentrate on tangerines and tangelos.

In the produce business, we often use the name tangerine and tangelo interchangeably, although they are different.

"Tangerine" is used to describe the smallest member of the mandarin family. The name "tangelo" is used to describe the larger tangerines. The tangelo is the end product of the crossing of various citrus fruits with the tangerine. Tangelos are much larger than tangerines, but the skin is tight, which makes them much harder to peel. In Florida there are four varieties of tangelos grown. The **Minneola** is the one I recommend. It is also known as the Red Tangelo and the Honeybell. Minneola are seedless, quite juicy, and very flavorful. This fruit is deep orange in color and much larger than the tangerine, and it has a rather pointed stemmed end which makes it easy to identify. I think the Minneola is one of the best citrus fruits of all.

The other three Florida tangelos are the **Early K,** the **Nova,** and the **Orlando Tangelo.** The Early K is the first tangelo available each year—its season begins in October and ends mid November. The Early K looks very much like a tangerine; it's very juicy, and has seeds, but the flavor makes me think of medicine. The season for the Novas and Orlando Tangelos begins in November; these varieties look just like the Early K, have about the same amount of seeds and juice, but are much sweeter than the Early K.

Tangerines are the baby of the mandarin family. The size may be "baby," but the flavor is delicious. Of all the citrus groups, the tangerine has the best overall flavor. Most of the tangerines sold in the United States come from Florida. The two most popular varieties are **Dancy** and **Robinson.** Dancy is the smaller of the two, but it also has the sweetest flavor.

The Dancy and the Robinson are very good, and I'm sure you will enjoy both, but there are two other tangerines to put on your must-taste list: **Murcott** and the **Clementine.** In 1972 the name Murcott was changed to Honey Tangerine. The name fits the fruit; it's sweet as honey, and the flesh is beautiful. The skin color never becomes a total orange, but don't let that stop you from choosing this wonderful tangerine. Next is the Clementine. I really like tha name, and the fruit even more. The Clementine is seedless, with a delightful flavor and a fine smooth texture.

When shopping for tangerines and tangelos, don't worry so much about color, especially with Florida fruit. Because of the warm nights, the fruits almost never reach a deep orange color. The peel should be nice and tight with no sagging at the stem end, a sign of age. Also avoid fruit with dark or mold spots. Tangerines and tangelos are quite perishable, so handle with care. They should be stored in the refrigerator (up to a week) until you are ready to eat.

Like the entire citrus family, tangelos and tangerines are high in vitamin C, and contain fair amounts of vitamin A and potassium.

VEGETABLES

Artichokes

The artichoke is native to the Mediterranean region of southern Italy. After its cultivation it not only became a favorite crop for Italian farmers but also became very popular at meal-time throughout the country. In fact, to this day Italy remains the top-producing as well as the top-consuming country of fresh artichokes in the world. However, it was French settlers who introduced the artichoke to America, in the Louisiana Territory. The French learned through Catherine de Medici of the unusual vegetable (which resembles a pine cone but is actually the flower of a plant related to the thistle). When Medici left Italy to become Queen of France, she was concerned about not finding Italian culinary delights in her new country, so the new queen not only brought Italian chefs with her to France, she also brought many food staples that they prepared, one of which was the artichoke. Thus began a new era in French cuisine.

Although Italy leads the world in production the best artichokes are grown right here in the United States—on the West Coast, about seventy miles south of San Francisco in the town of Castroville, California. Thanks to warm days and cool, foggy nights and mornings, the nut-like flavor of Castroville's artichokes is surpassed nowhere on earth.

Artichokes are available year round; however, the peak season for flavor runs March through May.

In selecting artichokes, choose whatever size you prefer. I love the baby artichokes that you can eat whole, including the chokes. The choke is the inedible thorny part between the paddles (leaves) and the heart, but it's so small on the baby artichokes that it is not noticeable. I also love the big ones because the heart is so much larger, and the heart is the best part. Choose artichokes that are heavy for their size, with tight heads. Don't worry if brown spots are present; most of the time they are caused by frost, and have no bearing on the flavor.

As for the nutritional value of this unusual vegetable, the bad news is that they are rather high in sodium. The good news is that artichokes are loaded with potassium and phosphorus as well as two vitamins that may surprise you, A and C.

Artichokes can be served hot or cold, with or without sauce or butter. If you want to cook them, it's easy. Just steam artichokes as you would broccoli or cauliflower, but longer, about forty minutes. Most people think eating the vegetable is the hard part. Nonsense! All you do is pull off a leaf, dip it in sauce, and drag it between your teeth, discarding the portion that does not come off. The tiny inner leaves may be eaten entirely, and they are quite good. After all leaves have been removed, you will see a fuzzy center called the choke. This portion is not edible (except in baby artichokes); scoop it out with a spoon and discard it. Be careful not to dig too deep, though, because beneath the choke is the real prize, the heart, the most flavor-packed part of the artichoke.

Arugula

Rocket salad, another name for arugula, was, and still is, an important vegetable crop in the areas of the world it is native to, southern Europe and western Asia. The original name of the vegetable is *eruca sativa,* so where does the name of arugula come from, you wonder? After becoming one of the most popular salad greens throughout the Old World, *eruca sativa* made its way to Brazil, where it became just as popular and was called "rucula." In America there have been minor changes in spelling and pronunciation to come up with "arugula." Unfortunately arugula, although very popular in Italian-American neighborhoods, has yet to gain the widespread popularity it deserves. Arugula has a distinct flavor, pungent and tangy, that I really enjoy. Try fresh arugula in your next tossed green salad. This vegetable mixes well with tomato, raw or cooked.

As I said, arugula has yet to gain widespread popularity on its own, but there is a new salad mixture on the gourmet scene called mescloon, which not only utilizes the beautiful green arugula leaves, (which resemble oversized oak leaves in appearance or the green leaf attached to radishes), but also contains the attractive yellow flower of the mature arugula plant. I first became aware of mescloon while living and working in New York, but my appreciation for this somewhat decadent mixture came on a recent visit to northern California. The mescloon mixture consists of the finest young and tender baby lettuces, such as red and green oak, Boston, red and green leaf, Lollo Rosso, Biando Rosso, Mizuna (a Japanese baby lettuce), and other expensive salad greens, such as arugula and its flower. During that California visit, I had the opportunity to dine at the exquisite Kenwood Restaurant, located in the Sonoma Valley, and on the recommendation of the manager and my dear friend, Jerry Cabral, I tried their house salad, featuring mescloon and sautéed goat cheese. The salad was divine!

When shopping for rocket salad or arugula, (in some stores you may see it labeled Italian watercress), freshness is the key. Choose whole leaves high in rich, green color, with no wilting around the edges. The vegetable is quite perishable, so try to purchase it on the day you plan to prepare it. Remember that because of the strong, pungent (but not overpowering) flavor, a little goes a long way. If you have to store arugula, wash it first in cold water, then wrap it in damp paper towels. Place that in a plastic bag, then refrigerate for no more than two days.

Like the other green leaf vegetables, arugula is very high in vitamin A, phosphorus, and calcium. However, because of the small amount you will be consuming, I think the flavor is the biggest selling point.

Asparagus

In the produce business, we refer to this vegetable as "grass." The word "asparagus" in the ancient Greek tongue meant "shoot." A member of the beautiful lilly family, asparagus is believed to have originated in Asia Minor or the eastern Mediterranean, two areas where this vegetable can still be found growing in its most primitive form.

During the heyday of the Roman Empire, asparagus was not only valued for its heavenly flavor, it was equally valued for its medicinal powers. The Romans believed asparagus could cure toothaches and heart ailments, among other things. They had many recipes and potions using fresh and dried asparagus. The farmers also worked hard to improve their cultivation techniques and kept extensive records of their progress.

For produce people, asparagus used to be the first sign of spring, making a light debut late in February. By the end of April, or by mid-May, the crop was at full tilt, winding down by the end of July. Today, with improved refrigeration, jet shipments from the southern hemisphere, and stronger varieties, asparagus is available year round. During January, the bulk of the asparagus sold in the United States comes from Chile, Mexico, and New Zealand. In February, the first domestic crop comes on line from California, where the season stretches through summer. During mid-summer, Washington and Michigan crops are available. Toward the end of fall, a second Mexican crop is available, taking up the slack when the domestic asparagus plays out. Through the remainder of fall, and part of winter, Chile and New Zealand asparagus are again sold.

There are two types of asparagus available, the *green* and *white* (actually off-white). The only real difference is in the color. The white aspargus is kept in darkness to prevent photosynthesis, whereas the green asparagus is grown in full sunlight. The taste of each type is virtually identical.

When shopping for fresh asparagus, always choose stalks that are straight and rich in color. The tops should be closed tightly. Some people prefer large asparagus, but personally, I've found the smaller the stalk, the better the flavor, and the vegetable is less stringy. When asparagus is past its peak, it will let you know. The tops will be open and if there is a slight foul odor, avoid the vegetable.

Store the asparagus no more than five days in the refrigerator in a tightly closed paper bag. Try to use it within three days of purchasing.

Asparagus is extremely nutritious: high in vitamins A, B, and C. It is also rich in calcium, protein, and potassium.

Beans

I guess we could say beans are truly the international vegetable, for they are grown in virtually every country on earth. There are dozens of varieties of beans, and each seems to have a different homeland.

Africa has been home to the *fava bean* for centuries. This large, flat bean is often called "horse bean" or "broad bean" in America. They sometimes grow to lengths of twenty inches. I had always thought they were native to Italy because there are many great Italian fava dishes, such as this one:

Fava Beans

Ingredients:
   2 pounds shelled fava beans
   3 tbs. margarine or olive oil
   1 clove garlic chopped fine
   1 small onion chopped
   1 lb. Jerusalem artichokes

Instructions:
   Boil fava beans until tender, about one to two hours.
   Drain, let cool. In frying pan, add margarine or
   oil, garlic, and onions. Cook until onions are trans-
   parent. Add artichokes and cook until golden
   brown, about ten to fifteen minutes. Now add
   fava beans. Cook until they are thoroughly heated.
   Add salt and pepper to taste, then serve.

The North and South American continents are home to *lima* and *snap beans* (or green beans), two of my favorites. When I was a child Mama called green beans "string beans." As I grew older I found out that everyone else called them string beans as well because of the string-like fiber that runs down the seam of the bean, which must be removed before cooking. But with today's hybrid varieties, strings are no longer a bother. The ten-to-twelve-inch long, flat, improved *Kentucky Wonder* variety is very popular in fresh and frozen markets. Some other favorites are the round *Blue Lake* and *Harvester*. They grow to be about half the size of the Kentucky Wonder, but I think their flavor is a little smoother, and their texture is less tough.

There are other snap beans to look for in the '90s. First, there's the *Yellow Wax Bean.* Except for color it can be a twin to the Blue Lake. These beans were once quite popular, then were pushed aside, and now they are making a comeback as a gourmet item.

The second to look for is the *Purple Snap.* With the ever-increasing American fancy for colorful foods, the purple snap is destined to be a hit. The flavor and texture are very similar to those of the Yellow Wax and Blue Lake beans, and they also make a great conversation piece at dinnertime or parties.

The *Lima bean* is an old American favorite. On a national scale, fresh lima beans are almost a thing of the past (why is a mystery to me), but in the South they are still quite popular during summer. If you are able to find them, those of you outside of the southern region, give them a try. You will truly enjoy the unique flavor and texture of these beans.

Chinese long beans (see Oriental vegetables) of course originated in Asia. Here in America they are sometimes called "yard-long beans."

Romano, or Italian beans, in the South called "bush beans." These beans have a wild look and are irregular in shape: some are flat, some are wide, and some are even curled—but all are tasty. They are wonderful cooked with chicken stock and diced onions. The Italian bean grows to about seven inches long. They are very popular internationally, but in America are popular only in the South.

Cranberry beans are one of the most beautiful to look at, and very tasty. In Mexico and the West Indies they are a huge favorite. The pod looks like something Andy Warhol would have designed: it's off-white and speckled, with pinkish red tints—just beautiful. Then when you open up the pod, the beans match the pods in color, though sometimes they are a little more red than white.

Fresh cranberry beans start to appear in August. Try this recipe:

CRANBERRY BEANS

Ingredients:
> 2 to 3 lbs. shelled cranberry beans
> 1 med. onion chopped
> 2 cloves garlic, chopped
> 2 med. tomatoes, chopped
> 2 tbs. olive oil
> salt and pepper to taste.

Instructions:
> In boiler place all ingredients, add 2 quarts of water. Cook over medium heat until beans are tender, about 2 hours, and of course, season to taste.

These beans are more familiar in their dried form, called "red beans," which are very popular in Louisiana.

Another variety is the **haricots verts,** or **French beans,** which look like miniature snap beans. When I was growing up, I had this type of bean in canned form, which can't touch fresh French beans when prepared properly. Now you may have to go to a gourmet shop or farmers' market to find fresh *haricots verts,* but it is well worth the adventure.

Beans are well rounded, being a good source for vitamins A, riboflavin, and a wealth of minerals, as well as being low in fat.

When shopping for fresh beans, of any variety, let your eye and touch be the guide. Look for fresh beans—those that have good color and no dark spots on either end. The bean should feel soft, almost moist. You never want to select stiff or hard beans, for those are two sure signs of age.

Fresh beans are fairly perishable, and they should be used as soon as possible. However, if stored properly in a tightly-closed paper bag, they will keep for up to a week in your refrigerator. Most beans are available year round. Bush beans may not be available in the winter, but most of the other types are.

Beets

Now here is a vegetable the American consumer has all but forgotten. Before the days of high-speed refrigerated trucks and air cargo planes, which get our fresh produce from source to retail outlet in days, and some cases hours, retailers were more dependent on local or regional suppliers and of course product availability was seasonal. In those days, beets were popular with retailers because they could be sold with their green tops during spring, summer, and fall and the sweet beet root was available during the coldest months of winter. Now, however, although beets are still a major crop in this country (the vegetable is grown in more than thirty states), the majority of those crops is sold to processors to be bottled or canned and used on salad bars nationwide.

In kitchens of days gone by, fresh beets were prized for several reasons. First, taste. The pleasant sweetness goes very well with meats and other vegetables. Today, with the new hybrid beets, the flavor is even better, so if shoppers would just try fresh beets, I'm sure this vegetable's popularity would soar as in the early years of this century. Also available are baby beets, which are absolutely delicious and make great conversation pieces at dinner parties when served raw on a vegetable tray. *Candy Cane* and *Golden* are two baby varieties.

Another reason why beets were so popular is that their green tops are an excellent substitute for spinach, cooked or in salads. (Many Europen restaurants distinguish between the beet roots and the beet tops, something I would like to see American restaurants do. There are many wonderful recipes with beet tops as well as beet roots).

When shopping for fresh beets always select firm, medium to small vegetables because the larger the beet the more likely it is to be dried out or woody in texture. The tops should be bold green and of course not wilted. After purchasing, remove the green top from the beet roots because those tops could extract moisture from the roots, which would cause them to dry out.

As for nutrition, beets are loaded; they are high in calcium, phosphorus, and protein. Indeed, we could call beets the blood food, for they furnish many nutrients needed to build red blood corpuscles.

Broccoli

The second most popular member of the cabbage family, and one of the most popular vegetables over all, is broccoli. This vegetable is another of the old-timers. The ancient Greeks and Romans are credited with its cultivation some two thousand years ago. From Italy broccoli was introduced to France, then England, then on to the New World. Although this vegetable was brought to America early in its history, it took some 150 years to transform broccoli from an ethnic Italian vegetable to the mainstream produce we think of today. In 1920 a group of farmers, led by the D'Arrigo brothers in northern California, decided to ship a sample load of broccoli back east, as well as to advertise this wonderful nourishing produce through the new craze of that era—radio. Since then, broccoli popularity has steadily grown.

California is by far the largest producer of the produce I called, as a child, "baby trees." That state's output accounts for over 85 percent of the annual broccoli crop marketed in America, and I have to give California an overall edge as far as quality is concerned, too. It seems that the area between San Francisco in the north and Santa Barbara in the south, with its warm days and fairly cool nights, is perfect for broccoli cultivation.

Other states that produce commercial broccoli include Arizona, Oregon, and Texas. Over the past few years I have seen steady improvement in the Texas crop, and the price is always competitive. Don't be afraid to ask produce people where their broccoli comes from.

There are two key factors to consider when shopping for fresh broccoli: touch and appearance. Always choose firm, heavy broccoli that has a nice green color with buds or florettes that are tightly compact. Some varieties have a purple tint, which is a sign of quality. Avoid broccoli that is limp and whose florettes have started to open or that has yellow flowers in the top. These are signs that the broccoli has passed its flavorful peak and has lost much of its valuable nourishment. Broccoli is fairly perishable, so it should be used within three days after purchasing. Broccoli, like other members of the cabbage family, is an excellent source for vitamins A and C.

Brussels Sprouts

Brussels sprouts are the newest member of the cabbage family. They were first discovered about three hundred years ago, and the name gives away their place of origin, Brussels, Belgium.

When I was a child I always thought this vegetable came from a strange cabbage that had little baby cabbages growing all around it. I must say I enjoyed looking at them much more than I did eating them. Now, after having seen the plant growing in the fields near Monterey, California, and Long Island, New York, I think they remind me more of a collard stalk, except that there aren't as many greens at the top, and all up and down the base of the plant there are rows filled with what look like miniature cabbages. I guess my childhood imagination was pretty good, except that instead of the cabbages being on the ground, they are on the stalk.

According to the experts, here is how to buy them. The smaller the sprout the better the taste; with Brussels sprouts anything over two to two and a half inches in diameter is considered too large. Always choose firm vegetables with a nice green color, and avoid those with wilting yellowish leaves, black spots, or little holes in the sprout. These are all signs of age or indications that insects may have infected that particular vegetable. One last note about choosing Brussels sprouts: put your nose to work. Overly mature vegetables give off a very strong odor, much like spoiled cabbage.

As for nutrition, Brussels sprouts are loaded—high in vitamins A, B, and C, high in protein, and low in calories. They have a low fat count and are an excellent source for calcium, iron, and potassium.

Cabbage

The cabbage is one of the most ancient vegetables grown today. Its cultivation dates back four thousand years, yet it remains among the top in popularity and sales to this date. Some one million tons are sold a year in the United States alone, and the only vegetables we buy in greater quantities are potatoes, lettuce, and tomatoes.

Head cabbage comes in two colors: **green** and **red,** sometimes called purple. There is no variety of white cabbage. I once got a phone call from someone raised in upstate New York. She was upset because she could not find New York white cabbage down South. I explained to her that there was no variety of white cabbage. What she was looking for was stored cabbage.

Green cabbage is sometimes called "new cabbage" in produce circles, because of the new green leaves that cover its head. As green cabbage ages, its color tends to fade. Now in the farm areas of New York State, and other northern farm regions where the winters are cold, it is a common practice to store cabbage in cold, dark barns. When this (old) cabbage reaches the market in the dead of winter, it is hard as a rock and almost bleached white. This old cabbage is great in cole slaw and for boiling, or anything else you would use the new green cabbage for, though its nutritional value may not be as high because of the aging factor.

Fresh cabbage may be as nourishing as any other single fruit or vegetable. It is an excellent source for calcium, phosphorus, and potassium, plus vitamins A, B, and C. (Remember: to receive the most nourishment from fresh vegetables, they should be consumed raw.)

During the cooler months, when lettuce prices soar upward, is an excellent time to try a **fresh cabbage salad.** Here is one I highly recommend: *shredded cabbage, red or green, with apples, using fresh-squeezed orange juice as your dressing. Of course, you could add some nuts to that salad for crunch and added protein.*

When selecting fresh cabbage, always choose firm heads that are heavy for their size. Stay away from cabbage that the produce person has trimmed. Cabbage is high in vitamin C, but each time it is cut or trimmed, some vitamin C is lost.

Napa Cabbage

Napa cabbage is sometimes called "Chinese cabbage," because until a few years ago, fresh napa could only be found in Oriental markets. Its other common name is "celery cabbage," although this vegetable does not resemble celery at all, in taste or appearance.

I myself use this vegetable quite often; it's fantastic raw or cooked. Raw napa is a great addition to any tossed salad. In fact, I suggest making your next tossed salad with napa and no lettuce at all, along with your other salad mixings. You'll find a pleasant sweet taste in this dish. As a cooked vegetable, napa blends well with other foods, especially chicken and potatoes, and it makes a nice coleslaw.

Nutrition and health experts believe eating cabbage helps prevent certain cancers. Napa is high in vitamins C and D. Although it has a sweet taste, it is lower in calories than the more familiar head cabbage

When selecting napa cabbage, choose cabbage that feels heavy and the leaves should have a nice, fresh appearance, with no bruises. Napa cabbage looks like romaine lettuce, but it is a lighter green in color.

Carrots

This ancient vegetable was being cultivated hundreds of years before the birth of Christ, but its exact origin is unknown. Various sources say Afghanistan, Japan, and the Mediterranean. Whatever their origin, for centuries carrots have been popular the world over.

Today's American consumer knows the carrot as a common vegetable that, if you want to spice them up a little, you purchase with the green tops attached. Well, let this greengrocer tell you, carrots are not so ordinary. They have quite a colorful past, which is still present in some other parts of the world. The early Dutch farmers grew large purple carrots, and the present-day farmers of northern Africa and Egypt still cultivate a small version of that variety, which I'm sure will be available in American markets soon. Other European farmers of the fifteenth century grew yellow carrots. During the sixteenth century the orange carrot made its debut in England and almost instantly became a food staple. The English women not only used the carrot as food: sixteenth-century trendsetters thought the green carrot tops were so attractive that they used them to decorate their hats and often braided them into their hair.

The first Europeans to settle in America were pleasantly suprised to find carrots a well-established crop in their newfound homeland. In fact, if they had not had carrots to eat during the brutal winter of 1609, the people of Jamestown, Virginia, would have starved.

Today carrots remain a popular vegetable; however, I think sales would soar if growers and processors would do just a little more marketing. We all know carrots are great in salads and as vegetable sticks, but not many realize what a wonderful cooked vegetable they are. Try these easy ideas: sliced carrots sautéed in butter and brown sugar, or steamed with salt, pepper, and fresh dill. For you meat eaters, next time you broil beef or pork, do it on a bed of carrots (you can also cook chicken and fish that way), but remember to drain off the fat before eating.

Carrots are available in retail stores every day of the year. The best quality come from California, the next best from Arizona, then Texas. Those three states are in production twelve months a year. Florida is another large producer of carrots, but I'm not a big fan of that sunshine crop; often the carrots are bitter, with a wood-like texture. During spring and summer other eastern states and Canada produce market-quality carrots, but they aren't nearly as sweet as the western carrots.

Remember your mother saying "Eat all your carrots so you can see well"? A single carrot six to eight inches long will supply over six thousand units of vitamin A, well above the daily recommended requirement. This vitamin is essential in developing strong bones and teeth as well as maintaining healthy eyes. Carrots also contain vitamins B, C, D, E, and K, and remain low in calories, about forty calories per carrot.

When shopping for carrots choose firm, clean vegetables no bigger than eight inches long and two inches in diameter. If tops are attached, remove them as soon as possible, because they will draw moisture from the carrot, causing bitterness and drying. Then place the carrots in a plastic bag and store in your refrigerator. Unfortunately, most carrots today are sold in prepackaged one and two pound colored plastic bags. Do yourself a favor and peek through the bag, making sure there is no sprouting at the top of the carrot, and no wilting at the bottom end. Both are signs of age.

Over the past ten years I've seen an increase in the popularity of the miniature carrots (about three inches long). In some areas—New York and Los Angeles, for instance—they're called French or Belgian carrots. There is nothing new about them; it's just that we Americans have finally caught up with the Europeans in appreciating smaller vegetables. Any of the recipes for standard carrots will work with the miniature ones, and I do think miniature carrots are much better cooked than raw.

Cauliflower

The word "cauliflower" means "cabbage flower" and this vegetable is the most elegant and delicate member of the cabbage family. For those reasons, it is also the most expensive. I say the cauliflower is elegant because it is so pleasing to look at. The beautiful snow-white or ivory inner portions of the vegetable are referred to as the curd. During the '90s that term may have to be dropped because other varieties of cauliflower are being developed that produce *green* and *purple* heads. The flavor of these is just as pleasing as that of the familiar snowball varieties.

The *white* varieties account for over 90 percent of all the cauliflower sold in the United States. There are a couple of reasons why I feel the colorful varieties will make drastic cuts into those percentages and will help cauliflower rival broccoli for the position of second most popular member of the cabbage family. First, cooking time is less for the green and purple cauliflower than the white—about the same as for broccoli. Second, we Americans are truly colorful people. During the '80s, although cauliflower has been around as long as broccoli (some twenty centuries), it was as if we had just discovered the vegetable. Now that we have discovered it and like it, the next step is to add colorful cauliflower to our evening meals, our vegetable crudités (raw vegetables), and our salads.

If you are wondering why I describe cauliflower as delicate, I ask, How many vegetables do you know of that need to wear a jacket? When cauliflower is being raised in the field, its white curd is blanketed by green leaves. That is called the jacket, which protects the delicate inner portion from the hot, dry sunlight of day and the cool, sometimes freezing temperatures at night. Because of the vegetable's delicacy, it takes a very good farmer to raise a marketable cauliflower, and that is why it is the most expensive member of the cabbage family.

The green leaves of the cauliflower jacket are edible. Their flavor reminds me of collard greens. When I worked out of the South San Francisco Produce Market, which is relatively close to the Salinas Valley, a major production area of cauliflower, I was able to purchase what was called "naked cauliflower." Naked cauliflower is untrimmed, with its jacket fully attached and free of the familiar plastic wrap we see in the supermarket. I wish for the consumer's sake that packing houses would ship some of the naked cauliflower to markets east of California so that easterners could enjoy those wonderful greens attached to the cauliflower.

Like the other members of the cabbage family, cauliflower is extremely nutritious, being high in both vitamins A and C, yet low in calories, as long as you do not add butter to steamed cauliflower. This vegetable is also a good source for iron, phosphorus, and calcium.

When shopping for cauliflower, you probably will not find the naked pack, but if you do, look for a colorful jacket—green with a clean white center that leads to the base of the vegetable. Pull back the jacket to inspect the curd, making sure it is tightly packed. When the curd starts to spread that is a sign of age. For the more familiar plastic wrapped cauliflower, choose a firm vegetable that has high color—clean white or ivory in the snowball varieties, nice green or purple in the colored varieties. If brown or dark spots are present, that vegetable should be discarded, as these are signs of age. One other tip: to be sure you have selected a fresh cauliflower, turn the package over and press the bottom stem. If it is soft, that is another sign of age.

Cauliflower will keep up to a week in the refrigerator, but for best flavor and nutrition, try to to consume it within three days of purchasing.

Chayote

I've got a feeling this vegetable is going to be very popular in the '90s. In Latin America,where chayote originated, some call it "pear vegetable" because of its shape and semisweet taste, but I think it looks more like an avocado. In other parts of South America the vegetable is called "mango squash"; like the mango it has one flat seed that adheres tightly to the flesh that surrounds it. The Cajuns and Creoles of Louisiana refer to it as *melleteu*. A Louisiana native said to me "*melleteu* grows like weeds down here so we cook it with everything."

Although the taste is semisweet, I doubt you would enjoy raw chayote by itself, though it is good used in salads or for dipping and it mixes well with other foods, complementing their flavor. It is also delicious sautéed with beef, chicken, or fish, and it does not lose its crunchiness after being cooked.

When shopping for chayote choose firm vegetables that are rich in color (nice green) and free of bruises.

Being a tropical vegetable, chayote is available virtually year round, with its peak season being October through March. To give you more cooking ideas, these vegetables are usually marketed with a recipe attached.

Chayote provides vitamin A and some potassium and is very low in calories. This squash stores well; it can be kept up to a week, unwrapped, in the refrigerator.

Corn

Corn is one of the true American food crops. Maize (the Native American name for this grain) originated in South America and was well established throughout the Americas long before the first European settlers ventured west. I read that Columbus and his crew members were astonished to see corn growing in fields that spread nearly ten miles and sometimes larger. The taste of this new-found grain was also a pleasure for the crew members. One other pleasant surprise for the men who sailed the Nina, Pinta, and Santa Maria was cigars made by Native Americans, using corn husks as wrappers.

Getting back to the first settlers, the Pilgrims were introduced to maize almost as they climbed off the *Mayflower*. In fact,they named the crop "Indian corn." Later that was shortened to simply "corn," which in Europe means "grain." The very trusting and friendly natives taught the Pilgrims everything they knew about planting maize, fertilizing it by using fish, havesting it, grinding it into flour, and saving and storing seed to plant the following season. It makes you wonder. If those Native Americans had a crystal ball, would they have been so willing to teach the settlers everything they knew about the amazing grain crop?

Today, hundreds of varieties of corn are grown in this country alone, and those crops are a long way from the wild grasses related to wheat and barley that sprang up in South America in pre-Columbian days. Although there are numerous varieties, from a commercial standpoint there are only two types: *field corn,* which is allowed to stay on the stalk and dry before harvesting and is used in making flour, corn oil, and feed for livestock as well as seed for future crops; and *sweet corn,* which is the type we buy fresh, frozen, and in cans.

Frankly, I don't think the variety is very important. I know we all have our regional favorites, like **Silver Queen** or **Golden Bantam** or **Country Gentleman,** but unless you know the farmer, and then the shipper and the wholesaler, I doubt you will know the exact variety that is in your retail outlet.

So what do you look for when shopping for fresh corn? First, ask your produce person what date the corn arrived; if it was more than three days ago, pass. Next, examine the husk for color. It should be evenly green, with no darkness at the bottom. That is a sign of age. The top should be free of worm holes or decay. Don't worry about the golden silk, because if it gets just a little moisture on it, it will blacken or fall off. Finally, pull back the ear to examine the kernel. Do not squeeze the kernels with your finger, for that will damage that ear of corn. Just examine the kernel carefully to see if it is plump and full. When corn starts to dry out, it sags at the top and there are dents that are noticeable in the top portion of that kernel.

Fresh corn is available year round, but the peak season begins late May and runs through September.

As soon as corn is picked, the sugar begins to convert into starch, so wait until peak season, June or July, to try one of my favorite ways to enjoy corn—raw. There is nothing as good as one of those sweet, yellow ears of corn, so plump and juicy.

Generally, fresh corn should be purchased on the day you are going to use it, unless you intend to freeze it.

As for nutrition, corn is well rounded, providing fair amounts of both vitamins A and B plus riboflavin, calcium, and phosphorus. Some may think it's a bit high in calories, about one hundred per ear.

Eggplant

Eggplant is one of a few vegetables not at its nutritional best when eaten raw. In fact, eggplant should never be consumed raw since it is a member of the nightshade family, which includes some poisonous plants. Raw eggplant could cause illness.

This subtropical jewel originated centuries ago in India and China, where it remains extremely popular today. Arabian traders took the vegetable westward to Turkey, where it spread to Greece and then to Spain and in the sixteenth century made its way to Italy. Eggplant seeds are believed to have been brought to America by Spanish explorers; whatever the case, eggplant found the southern part of this country an ideal growing area. That explains why Florida was and still is the number one producer of eggplant in the United States.

There are many varieties of eggplant: in the common globe shape there are *New York, Black Magic,* and *Black Beauty* eggplants. They all are deep purple, almost black in color. The medium globe or Italian eggplant has that same color but is about half the size of the common varieties; other medium eggplants include, the *French Bonde de Valence,* a medium round eggplant; *Puertician Rayada,* a purple and white striped eggplant, and *Italian Rosa Bianco,* another purple and white one. Some of the white varieties, which come in all shapes and sizes are the *Chinese, Casper, White Egg, Easter Egg,* and *Thia Round Turtle Egg.* Then there are the green varieties, which are also egg-shaped; my two favorites are the *Applegreen,* about the size of a small Granny Smith apple, and the *Green Thia,* which comes in bunches and looks like green grapes.

Although there are many types of eggplant, they have only three basic differences: shape, color, and size. Some will argue that the flavor is different in the smaller eggplant, but I feel the major difference between the small and large eggplant is that the small ones have fewer seeds, which makes the texture smoother when cooked.

Being a subtropical vegetable, eggplant is available year round. When shopping, look for firm, bright, shiny eggplant that is free of scars or dark spots. When eggplant has been mistreated, it will tell (those dark spots), so avoid bruised eggplant. Another freshness sign is the stem end. First, it should always be on the eggplant, for if it has been removed, the retailer is trying to hide something—age, to be exact. Second, the stem should be richly green in color; if it is not, it too is old and should be avoided. That goes for all eggplant, including the white varieties.

For those of you trying to cut back on your red meat intake, eggplant is a great substitute. It offers a fair amount of protein, is low in calories, and is high in potassium, calcium, and phosphorus.

EASY EGGPLANT:

Ingredients:
> 2 med. eggplants
> 5 tbs. salt
> 2 tsp. minced garlic
> 1/2 cup oil
> 1/3 cup vinegar
> 1/3 cup white wine
> pepper

Instructions:
> Wash eggplant and remove cap. Cut into small pieces about 1" sq. Salt and let drain about 20 min. Pat dry and place in baking pan. Mix garlic with oil and pour over eggplant. Bake in preheated 400 degree oven until eggplant is tender and brown. Cool and place in bowl. Mix in vinegar, wine, and pepper to taste. Makes an excellent salad and is great with rice or pasta as a side dish or main dish.

Garlic

This member of the onion family is believed to have originated in Asia thousands of years ago. In addition to its ability to add excellent flavors to various cuisine, over the centuries mystic and curative powers have been attributed to garlic. Because Egyptians believed that eating garlic gave strength, it was fed to the workers who constructed the great pyramids. The Roman upper class did not care much for the smell of garlic, but they did supply it to Roman soldiers to eat and carry into battle to give them strength and courage.

As for the mystical stuff, I guess there are more stories connected with garlic than any other food item. In some parts of the world it is still believed that garlic can ward off evil spirits. This is true even in this country; in New Orleans, if you go into one of the voodoo shops on Bourbon Street, you'll see several potions and recipes calling for garlic to fight evil spirits. As for garlic's curative powers, there is some validity to that. In fact, in 1959 the Food and Drug Research Laboratory issued a statement proclaiming that garlic does have some healing abilities, something that many home doctors had known for centuries. The statement credited garlic with the ability to remove toxins from the body, which also helps reduce blood pressure, among other things.

There are basically three types of garlic. First is the *Creole* variety, and I'm sure you know which part of the country this one is most popular in. Creole garlic has the strongest flavor and smell. The skin color is totally white, and it may be marketed under the name American garlic. Next is the *Italian,* sometimes called the Mexican variety. You will know this type by the purplish skin color. The Italian garlic has a nice, mild flavor. Lastly is the *Tahitian* variety. It's the biggest of the three varieties, being two to three inches in diameter, and has more but smaller cloves. Recently, through cross-breeding, an *Elephant* variety has been introduced. It has the totally white skin of the Creole variety and the mild flavor of the Italian, yet it is twice the size of the Tahitian variety. Elephant garlic is excellent for baking, and its divided cloves are much easier to work with because of their enormous size.

Garlic is available year round. When shopping, avoid softness, sprouting, and wetness, which are sure signs of age. Always choose firm, dry garlic with paper-like skin. If stored properly, in a paper bag placed in a cool dry place, garlic will keep for at least a month at home. Remember to store this vegetable away from foods that could pick up its smells.

Greens

Chard

To look at *Swiss chard,* you wouldn't think that this vegetable is related to the beet, but it is. In fact, chard is the oldest member of the beet family; it just never evolved the large round roots as did its younger brother.

Chard is believed to have originated in Asia Minor, where two types were grown: light green and dark green. In other areas, such as the Near East and the Mediterranean region, a red chard grew. (Red chard is mentioned in ancient Greek writing.)

As for its name, Swiss chard, in the sixteenth century a Swiss botanist wrote a detailed report on the various types of chard, and ever since then, the agricultural world has referred to the vegetable as Swiss chard.

The Swiss chard is one of our most versatile vegetables. There are two edible parts, which can be prepared in a number of ways. First, the leaf portion can be cooked the same way we Southerners cook turnip greens, and unlike turnip greens, chard tops also make a wonderful salad. The other edible portion is the stem, which is the part consumed by most Americans who have discovered this ancient vegetable. When fresh the stem is beautiful in both the green and red varieties. On the green variety the stem is a milky white color, and the texture is crisp, like celery. For the red type the texture is the same, but the color is a cross between apple red and sunset orange. A note for you caterers: chard stems are excellent for your *plat de crudité* (raw vegetable platter). When served raw, chard has a beet-like flavor, but when steamed, the flavor reminds you of celery.

As for nutrition, chard, like its baby brother the beet, is loaded. It's high in vitamin A and contains large amounts of potassium and iron. As for calorie count, one cup of chard contains only about thirty calories.

Swiss chard is available year round. When shopping for it, choose bunches that are high in color—deep green in the green variety and rich, bold red in the red variety. The stems should be firm but not dried out, with no darkening at the bottom end. Chard should be bought no more than three days prior to using, wrapped in a damp paper towel and refrigerated.

Collards

Those of us born in the South have been familiar with this produce item ever since we were old enough to sit down for Sunday dinner. Collards are a non-head-forming member of the cabbage family, like kale. In fact, some experts say the only difference between the two is the curly leaves, although Southerners know better. Cooked kale is a fantastic dish, but it just does not compare to the flavor and body of properly prepared collard greens.

This plant has been around since prehistoric times, and it is believed to have originated in Asia, where reportedly wild collards still flourish. They were brought to this country during the fifteenth century and soon became a very popular winter vegetable because the cold seems to bring out the best flavor of the greens. Through the years their popularity has dropped off considerably in the North, but in the South they are just as popular as they were one hundred years ago. In fact, this region leads the nation in production and consumption of fresh collard greens.

Collards are available virtually year round; however, those with the best flavor are on the market during fall and winter. When shopping, choose vegetables rich in color (dark green) with firm stems. Avoid any greens with wilting or yellowing leaves. Like the other members of the cabbage family, collards are extremely nutritious. Large amounts of vitamin A and riboflavin are found within the dark green leaves.

Dandelion Greens

That's right. The green leaves from those little yellow flowers are edible, and, I might add, quite good and very nutritious. This member of the chicory family proves that one person's flower or weed is another person's gourmet salad—and it makes a nice cooked side dish also. The first time I was introduced to dandelion greens as a food was in New York City. The gourmet shop I worked at carried them, and they sold very well. I remember asking Charlie Balducci, "What's the story with dandelion greens?" After he explained the culinary appeal of the weed, I gathered some up, took them home, prepared them, and to my surprise I totally enjoyed them

Here is a little tip about cooking dandelion greens: Some people think that they are quite bitter, so when you cook them, pour the first water off, then cook them again, and that removes a lot of the bitterness. I think you will find they make a great substitute for spinach salad.

Dandelion greens are at their flavorful best during spring and early summer. When shopping, always choose rich, green leaves with no wilting or yellowing present. Dandelions are very nutritious. They are loaded with vitamin A, carbohydrates, calcium, and large amounts of riboflavin.

Turnip Greens

Turnips are believed to have originated in Russia, which makes sense because they do thrive in the cooler climates. However, they have a long history of cultivation in other parts of Europe, not only as food for humans, but as feed for livestock. Turnips made their appearance in North America during the mid-sixteenth century and have thrived since, especially in the South.

Turnip greens are not a separate vegetable, but an extension of the turnip roots, although many Americans buy them as such. When shopping for the greens, avoid any with yellowing or wilting leaves. After purchasing, store two to three days in the refrigerator in a paper bag. To revive the greens before cooking, plunge them into cold water before preparing. Traditionally Southerners cook their turnip greens with pork, but I think they taste much better if you substitute a chicken leg or back for the pork.

When turnip roots and greens are prepared together, there are very few vegetables that can equal the nutritional output. Vitamins A, B, C, E, and K are all present in this very nourishing dish.

Jerusalem Artichokes

The name "Jerusalem artichoke" is very misleading—the vegetable has no ties to Jerusalem, and it is not in the same botanical family as the artichoke, although the cooked flavor does bring to mind (or tastebuds) the flavor of cooked artichokes. A few years ago, someone decided to rename this vegetable "sunchoke" because in actuality it is the tube produced underground by a type of sunflower plant.

This choke is one of the few vegetables that is native to North America, and was a favorite of the Native Americans who inhabited this continent. On first sight, you might mistake Jerusalem artichokes for small Irish potatoes, and in fact, the Indians used this vegetable in much the same way the Irish immigrants used the potato. Beneath the tan-colored skin can be found a clean, fresh, white flesh that is crisp and has a nut-like flavor much like that of the Globe artichoke. But unlike that artichoke, Jerusalem artichokes can be eaten raw.

Jerusalem artichokes are available pretty much year round, but are at their peek during fall and winter. Choose sunchokes light in color that are firm to the touch and have no mold or decay. The Jerusalem artichoke (sunchoke) is an excellent source for vitamin B and iron.

Jicama

The exact origin of this vegetable is unclear; it grows wild in all the tropical zones of the world. Whereas in America the potato is king, in the tropics jicama wears the crown. Like the potato, the jicama is also the swollen root of a vine related to the morning glory family, and the flavors of potatoes and jicama are somewhat alike. However, the jicama contains much more water, and the average jicama sold in American produce markets is about the size of a small cantaloupe. The skin is a dark cardboard color, but inside you'll find beautiful white-colored flesh that is crisp and crunchy.

Unlike potatoes, jicama is great raw. I love jicama in salads, and it is also wonderful cut into sticks and served with dips. Jicama is the perfect substitute if you don't want to pay the high price for fresh water chestnuts, and keep in mind that it may be used in any recipe that calls for potatoes. You can boil it, bake it, and even fry it. You must try this marvelous tropical vegetable; I know you will love it.

Jicama is available year round in produce markets and the everyday grocery store, but this tropical treasure is at its tasteful best during our fall and winter. When shopping, avoid jicama with bruises or deep cuts. The vegetable will store uncut for weeks in the refrigerator. There is no need to bag it, but once cut it should be used as soon as possible.

The jicama contains a fair amount of vitamin C and is loaded with potassium, yet remains low in calories, about forty-five per eight ounces.

Kale

Today the primary use for this leafy vegetable is ornamental. American restaurants use this hearty, non-head-forming member of the cabbage family to decorate salad bars and fruit trays, and as garnish on serving plates. However, kale makes an excellent cooked vegetable and has been used as a food source for thousands of years. The cultivation of kale dates back so many centuries that its exact origin is unclear. It could be the Mediterranean region or Asia Minor. The ancient Greeks farmed kale, as did the Romans, and, later on, the French, who introduced it to the British. By the end of the fifteenth century kale was being grown in the New World, and has been a steady crop since. The only greens I enjoy more when cooked in the traditional southern style are collards. If you don't know how to cook kale, any recipe you have for collards, turnips, or other greens will do.

There are two main varieties of kale: the *Scotch* and the *Blue.* They are equal in flavor and nutritional value, but the Blue is a special favorite of restaurants because of its color tint.

Kale is available year round, like the other members of the cabbage family. When shopping, choose fresh-looking bunches. Be sure that the stemmed ends are clean, with no darkness, and that the leaves are fresh, with no wilting or yellowish color. As for nutritional value, kale is loaded with vitamins A, B, and C. There are also sufficient amounts of riboflavin, calcium, iron, and phosphorous contained in the luscious green and blue leaves of this vegetable.

Kohlrabi

In German the word *kohl* means "cabbage," and *rabi* means "turnip." Whereas most vegetables can be traced back to ancient times, the kohlrabi did not make its debut until the fifteenth century. It originated in Northern Europe and by century's end was being enjoyed throughout the continent of Europe.

The kohlrabi was introduced to America in the early 1800s and unfortunately, the vegetable has yet to gain the popularity it deserves. Kohlrabi looks like a root vegetable, but unlike root vegetables, whose globe portions grow underground, the kohlrabi globe forms and grows above ground. This round globe reminds me of an onion, though a different color.

In Europe there are many varieties of kolhrabi grown, but in America only two types are cultivated: *Early Vienna,* which is a light green color, and *Early Purple Vienna,* whose color is like that of a fresh beet.

If you enjoy the taste of fresh turnips and the greens but you can't handle too much of them at one time, the kohlrabi could be your answer. When cooked, kohlrabi has a mild turnip flavor. I'm sure if more Southerners would give this vegetable a try, its popularity would soar.

Kohlrabi has two edible parts. First, there is the green leafy portion, which can be cut off and cooked like spinach or other leaf vegetables. The second edible portion is the globe, whose possibilities are endless. It can be boiled as we do root vegetables, steamed the way you would prepare broccoli, or to make an elegant dish, cored and used in any stuffed mushroom recipe. Raw kohlrabi is as enjoyable as cooked, for it is crisp and juicy; try adding some to your next tossed salad. The purple kohlrabi is like having several vegetables in one, for not only can you cook both parts of the vegetable as suggested above, but the leaf portion also adds beautiful color to any decorative tray.

When shopping, choose young kohlrabi (size is the key; the globe should not be larger than 2-1/2 inches, about the size of a kiwi) that is fresh and full of color. Avoid kohlrabi with yellow and wilting leaves, and never choose kohlrabi whose globes are too large, for they can be tough and stringy.

As for the nutritional benefits of the kohlrabi, it is loaded. with nutrition. It is high in vitamin C, and the leaf portion contains large amounts of vitamin A. The kohlrabi is also an excellent blood cleanser and contains high amounts of calcium.

Lettuce

Lettuce is believed to have first been cultivated in Asia Minor and by the sixteenth century was a common vegetable throughout the contintent of Europe. On our continent, lettuce was one of the first vegetables planted by the early settlers, if not the very first. Nowadays lettuce, which has several varieties, rivals the potato for the number one spot in annual American vegetable sales and consumption. At least one variety of lettuce is grown in every state in the union, including Alaska and Hawaii. In fact, I tasted the best leaf lettuce of my life while visiting the island of Maui. It was grown in the same area famous for the Maui sweet onion—kula—just at the foot of the dormant volcano Haleakala.

As I said, one can find lettuce growing in every state. However, the majority of the commercially grown crops (more than 75 percent) is produced by California and Arizona. California is by far the largest single producer and, in my opinion, the producer of the world's best commercially grown lettuces. Arizona is a good second. This is not to snub the other production areas, but Salinas, California (an area just south of San Jose), has warm days and cool nights, which is perfect for lettuce, whereas in other commercial production areas such as Florida, Texas, and New Jersey, the nights are sometimes as hot as the days and the lettuce just is not as crisp and sweet as in California. However, I must say that over the past few years, I have noticed much improvement in those eastern lettuces.

There are dozens of varieties of lettuce, but only a few are grown commercially. First, there is crisp head lettuce—known to most consumers as *Iceberg* lettuce. The name "Iceberg" came from the way the lettuce used to be packed in the field for shipping. The vegetable was cut and trimmed, then placed in a crate with a layer of ice on top, then a layer of lettuce, and so on until the crate was full. This made for a pretty heavy crate, thus the name "Iceberg." Crisp head lettuce is by far the most popular salad green in America, although, in my opinion, it is far from the most tasty.

Romaine's flavor is as trendy as a BMW 325. Romaine is considered a head lettuce, although the leaves do not close together in a round ball; rather, they close long and flat. The outer leaves of romaine are a bold, dark green, while the inner leaves are a much lighter color and are sometimes even yellow.

In certain restaurants, especially on the West Coast, these golden inner leaves are prepared into separate salads altogether.

Green leaf has become quite a popular lettuce over the past five years. It is a beautiful, green, curly-leaf variety that really stands out in a salad mixture. In my opinion, though, the flavor is a little flat and the texture too coarse and grassy.

Red leaf lettuce is curly, like green leaf, but that is where the similarity ends. The tips are a dark auburn red color. Red leaf is my personal favorite; it has a soft texture and a mild, sweet taste. Red leaf not only tastes good but is quite pleasing to the eye.

Other leaf lettuces include *Boston* lettuce, also called butter leaf lettuce because of the soft, buttery flavor and texture; and *Bibb* lettuce, which the old timers referred to as limestone lettuce, according to Vick Korfhage of Korfhage Greenhouses in Louisville, Kentucky. Vick explains that Bibb lettuce grown in the limestone-laden fields of Kentucky has a distinct flavor of its own, and I agree. This lettuce looks like a miniature romaine, but the only thing small about it is its size—the flavor is outstanding, whether grown in Kentucky, upstate New York, or California.

Lettuce is available year round, but as consumers know, prices do tend to run on the high side during the winter months. However, something you may not realize is that if you divide the price of a head of lettuce into the per-serving cost, I'm sure you will find lettuce is still a good value, even in winter.

When shopping for lettuce of any variety, freshness is key. Never choose lettuce that has wilting or yellowing leaves. Another way to tell freshness is to inspect the base of the vegetable; it should always be hard and have a pale white to pinkish color. If you notice that the produce person has trimmed the base quite a bit, that, too, is a warning sign that the retailer is trying to pass off old lettuce. Lettuce can be stored up to four days in the refrigerator, but try to use it within three.

As for the nutritional benefits of lettuce, they're quite good, even for iceberg. They are good sources for vitamins A, B, and some C, plus riboflavin. What may surprise you is that lettuces are also good providers of calcium and potassium.

Mushrooms

The average consumer knows mushrooms as little white, umbrella-shaped items that are good in salads, make a nice soup, and are excellent when cooked into sauces with meats and/or other produce items. Worldwide over two thousand varieties of mushrooms are eaten on a somewhat regular basis, and that has been going on more than two thousand years. Egyptian kings declared mushrooms off limits to the under-class, as did the Roman leadership in the days of the Roman Empire, although any Roman citizen could eat the food of the gods on holy days.

Mushrooms have been harvested in small amounts as food for centuries, but it's the French who are credited with being the first to cultivate this culinary wonder on a commercial scale, during the latter part of the eighteenth century.

Mushrooms are totally fascinating to me; they're not an-chored by roots, and they don't bear flowers or leaves, not even seeds. In fact, mushrooms don't belong to the vegetable family. They are part of the fungi family, the same as the lowly but useful bread mold and yeast. Another member of the ill-sounding fungi family is the very expensive truffle.

In the United States, mushroom farming became an indus-try during the latter part of the nineteenth century in Pennsyl-vania. To this day that state still produces about half the mushrooms sold in this country annually. Back in the early days farming was done in caves and because mushrooms thrive in cooler temperatures the best quality and quantity was harvested in late autumn,winter, and early spring, with sup-plies dropping to zero in the heat of summer. Today's mush-room season is year round because the caves (mushroom houses) are man-made, and winter is constantly supplied by air conditioning. Over the past few decades, the white mushroom has become the most common type. That wasn't always the case. Before World War II, I'm told consumers only wanted the darker types; some of the old-time produce people tell me the brown varieties have an earthier flavor, and are just plain better. But the best mushrooms I have eaten were white ones that came from California.

Of the common *white* varieties of mushrooms that we find in the retail stores, about 95 percent are U.S. Number 1. This means that these mushrooms are of uniform shape, are disease-free, and have caps closed tightly around the stems. However, there is another grade—U.S. Number 2. In the produce business we call these mushrooms "mature." Since they are a bit older than the Number 1 mushroom, their caps are open. A large number of the Number 2 grade mushrooms are sold by wholesalers to pizza restaurants. Because of the age, Number 2 mushrooms contain less moisture and bake more easily—not to mention they sell at a much lower price.

Number 1 mushrooms are also divided into sizes, button being the smallest (under one inch diameter), then medium, large, and extra large or jumbo, which are over three inches in diameter.

The best mushrooms I ever ate came from the Petaluma Mushroom Farm, located about twenty-five miles east of Bodega Bay, California (the little town made famous in Alfred Hitchcock's movie *The Birds).* These mushrooms are just beautiful, the color is snow-white, and the shape is perfect. When I sliced into them I was so surprised to see pink gills (gills are the inside of the mushroom that is covered up by the cap). Never before nor since have I seen such a pretty inside of a mushroom, and the flavor was outstanding. If ever you are out in the San Francisco Bay area make a point to go into a retail store and ask if they have mushrooms from Petaluma Mushroom Farm. They make an excellent side dish sautéed with olive oil, white wine, and minced garlic.

When shopping for white mushrooms, most experts advise to select mushrooms with closed caps. I think it depends on what you are going to use them for. If they're to be eaten raw or sliced into salads, choose the closed cap Number 1, but if you plan to cook with the mushrooms, the Number 2 grade mature ones do have a more distinctive flavor. It's important to choose mushrooms that are firm, dry, and free of dark spots.

It's a shame that some retailers wet their mushrooms trying to enhance their appearance. As soon as they are taken from the cool produce section, they start to break down and become slimy. Always avoid slimy mushrooms. Remember that mushrooms are very perishable and should be used within two or three days after purchasing. If you have to store them, place the mushrooms in a paper bag before putting them in the vegetable bin. If moisture forms inside the bag, it will not fall back onto the mushrooms as easily as it would in a plastic bag.

As for nutritional value, mushrooms are quite earthy, thus a good source for iron, phosphorous, potassium, and calcium. They are low in calories and also contain small amounts of vitamins B and C.

Wild Mushrooms

These made their mark on the American gourmet scene during the '80s, and are worth mentioning. In Europe, Scandinavia, and other parts of the world, gathering wild mushrooms is a common hobby, but here in the states we have been discouraged from mushroom gathering. It takes an expert to tell if those beautiful wild mushrooms are safe and edible, or poisonous, even causing death. I have had a copy of the Audubon Society's *Field Guide To North American Mushrooms* for a couple of years and explore it on regular basis, but I have never gone out into the forest to pick wild mushrooms. I guess those warnings really hit home with me. However, in the Pacific Northwest, mushroom gathering is on the rise; many people have found a large profit awaiting them at the end of their mushroom explorations.Their gatherings are air-shipped to fancy restaurants and gourmet shops across the United States and to Canada.

There are so many varieties of wild and exotic mushrooms available that you could build a store around them alone. In New York's Balducci's the mushroom is not the centerpiece, but it is definitely a main attraction. On any given day no less than ten varieties of domesticated and wild mushrooms are available to shoppers, and on some days as many as twenty varieties are on hand. They come from Italy, France, Oregon, and the northeastern United States, as well as Canada. Of course these mushrooms sell at above premium prices, but considering the effort that goes into gathering, shipping, and preparing these mushrooms, the price is worth it, and the flavors are excellent.

Here are just a few of the wild mushrooms available in gourmet shops. The most expensive mushroom is the *Morel:* the last price I was quoted was $139.00 per pound. The color is dark gray, almost black, with a flavor that is quite earthy and very rich. The Morel looks like a natural sponge; in fact, one of its common names is "sponge mushroom."

The *Chantrelle* is as pretty as its name; this variety is a deep golden yellow color, with a shape reminding me of miniature daisies. The flavor and aroma are sweet like fresh apricots.

The *Enoki* is a very strange looking mushroom—tall, very thin, off-white in color with miniature caps about the size of a pencil eraser. The Enoki mushrooms are excellent in salads or cooked. They look like bean sprouts.

The *Shitake* mushroom is native to Japan and is as well known for the way it grows (on dead oak wood) as the wonderful flavor it yields. There is a mushroom farm in North Carolina that has begun to produce Shitake mushrooms as good as any from the Orient. In fact, Shitakes have become a common item in American stores over the past few years, and prices have dropped dramatically.

The *Oyster mushroom* is still popular with pickers in the wild, but has been domesticated over the past ten years. Oyster mushrooms grow in clusters in sawdust or other wood by-products as well as straw. They have an extremely wide color range, from white to gray and near black; their texture is always consistent—velvety smooth and their flavor resembles the seafood they were named for.

There is an Oyster hybrid called "Angel Trumpet." It is a clean, white mushroom. The shape is the instrument Miles

Davis plays. You could say the flavor of this mushroom leaves a delightful jazz note on your palate. Other wild mushrooms to look for and give a try include the **Italian Crommini,** or **Brown Field Mushroom.** It's called the father of the white commercial mushroom. Then there is the **Cep.** In the Norwegian language that word means "mushroom," but the Cep I'm talking of is a large white mushroom about the size of those old fashioned oatmeal cookies. Another variety is the **Porcino,** the classic Italian mushroom. It's very difficult to find a mushroom to surpass this one as far as flavor and appearance. Then the **French Pierrie de Mountain,** or foot of the mountain. This miniature golden brown mushroom is umbrella-shaped and fantastic for sautéing.

There are so many wild mushrooms out there waiting to be discovered, if you find any please drop me a line and share your find. Of course, wild mushrooms do sell for premium prices, but it doesn't take a lot of mushrooms to add a lot of flavor to your recipes.

Truffles belong to the same plant family as mushrooms— fungi. I just can't discuss mushrooms without mentioning truffels. The world's finest and most expensive truffles come from Italy's Piedmont Region and the Peerigord area of France. Unlike mushrooms, which spawn, then shoot upwards and grow above ground, truffles grow beneath the earth. To be exact, they grow underneath the root system of small birch or oak trees. Pigs are used to gather them, and the animal is able to unearth the truffle without causing damage. Truffles are mostly used by fancy restaurants or specialty shops and do come with very high price tags.

Okra

This ancient vegetable, a close relative to the cotton plant, originated in northeast Africa. I'm told it's not uncommon to see wild okra still growing today in Ethiopia and the upper Nile region.

Okra was, and still is, a staple in Africa, India, and the

Mediterranean area. The unique vegetable was brought to America along with human cargo in the hull of slave ships. Both ill-treated cargos survived harsh times in their new homeland and have made significant impacts on the culinary world.

In Africa, the words "okra" and "gumbo" are interchangeable. But in the United States, gumbo has come to mean a soup/stew associated with Creole cooking, and okra refers to the primary ingredient in its preparation.

In my eyes, okra, with its green color of spring grass and its intriguing cylindrical shape, is one of the most beautiful of vegetables. I've often asked myself whether I feel this way because the history of this ancient food and my own cultural history are so closely intertwined.

I grew up eating okra, and my grandfather, W. H. Curtis, raised the best I've ever tasted. Each summer morning, he and I would inspect the plants (that looked so much like the cotton plants he spent his days with), and harvest the ripe vegetables. Then we'd take them in to my grandmother Corine, who must have had fifty different ways to prepare the fruits (vegetables) of our labor: fried, boiled, cooked with onions or tomatoes in stews, pickled, or canned. She made hot ones, sweet ones, sour ones, and okra with herbs. If I had known then what I would be doing for a living, I would have written down everything Gramma did in her kitchen. Thank goodness my mama knows many of Gramma's secrets.

Okra is available year round; however, it's at its best during the hottest months of summer, July and August. When shopping, remember big okra is not good okra; that's what my grandfather would say. Choose vegetables no more than three inches long and one-half inch in diameter, that are free from scars and wetness. The stem end where the vegetable was cut from the plant should have a light color; if dark, the okra is old and should be avoided.

Okra will keep up to a week in the refrigerator, stored in paper bags in the vegetable bin, but try to use within three days of purchasing.

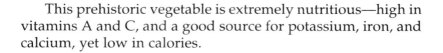

This prehistoric vegetable is extremely nutritious—high in vitamins A and C, and a good source for potassium, iron, and calcium, yet low in calories.

Oriental Vegetables

As recently as five to ten years ago, Chinese vegetables were thought to be strange or exotic, and were very hard to find outside the big-city Chinatown areas of San Francisco and New York. However, today things have changed. With the ever-increasing popularity of these items, many supermarket chains have designated large parts of their produce sections for Oriental vegetables, which taste great and are very nutritious—not to mention that they cook with relative ease in a short time, which is perfect for the America of the '90s.

Bean Sprouts. This vegetable has made the mainstream. Twenty years ago you couldn't pay most people to try bean sprouts, but now they are so popular that they are not even thought of as an Oriental vegetable. I guess the majority of bean sprouts used in this country are tossed into salads, but don't forget that when cooked they also make a wonderful vegetable.

Bittermelon (*foo gwa*). This is another vegetable used quite often in soups. I guess we could call it the Chinese cucumber. It is light green with bumpy grooves up and down the surface. Inside the flesh is white and pink, and quite attractive.

Bok Choy. This vegetable originated in Asia and has been a mainstay for centuries throughout the Orient, and is one of my favorite Oriental vegetables. Bok choy is very similar to Swiss chard; in fact, many people confuse the two vegetables. When fresh. bok choy, like the smaller Swiss chard, has beautiful, milky-white stalks with bold green leaves. Unlike Swiss chard, I don't recommend using the edible green tops of bok choy for fresh salads; when eaten raw, these greens have a hot, spicy taste that I just don't care for—and I don't know anyone else who enjoys it either. When cooked, though, the hotness seems to disappear and the tops become a nice vegetable for dinner. The stalks, however, are mild and can be eaten raw, although few people do since the texture is watery and quite crunchy. When steamed or sautéed, these stalks become much more tender and sweet. Sometimes baby bok choy is available. These little jewels can be cooked whole, steamed or boiled, and I highly recommend them. Bok choy is low in calories but high in both vitamins A and C, and contains large amounts of calcium. In fact, a cup of cooked bok choy provides as much calcium as a cup of milk.

The pointers for selecting bok choy are similar to those for selecting Swiss chard. Choose vegetables with good color and no darks spots. I recommend buying bok choy no more than three days prior to using. Wrap the vegetable in a damp paper towel and store in your refrigerator.

Chinese Longbean (*dow kok*). The first time I saw this vegetable was in the San Francisco Golden Gate Produce Terminal. I had no idea what it was. It looked like green pieces of rope, scrap pieces at that, about one foot long and about a quarter-inch in diameter, but I found that when cooked, these green beans are very tasty and tender, similar to the French haricots verts.

Chinese Mustard Green (*kai choy*). The bitterness is slightly stronger than the mustard green found in the American South. In Chinese cuisine it is most often featured in soups or as a stir-fry ingredient.

Chinese Okra (*sing gwa*). This vegetable could be called giant okra, as it is eight to twelve inches long and about an inch thick. The color is much deeper than we southerners are accustomed to seeing in our little okra, but its flavor reminds me of our own backyard okra.

Chinese Snow Pea, or ***Chinese Pea Pod.*** This is another of the Oriental vegetables that has worked its way into the American mainstream, and the only reason young Americans know of its Oriental origin is because of its name. Snow peas are by far the most popular of Oriental vegetables. They're great raw or cooked, and mix well with meat, fish, and other vegetables. Fresh steamed snow peas and sliced carrots makes an elegant dish; sautéed snow peas in white wine and butter are also fantastic.

The snow pea has a flat pod, unlike the English pea, and whereas the round, glossy green pod of English peas is inedible, the flat light green pods of snow peas are sweet and tender. The biggest difference most people think of between the snow pea and English pea is the price; English peas may sell for one dollar per pound and snow peas at two dollars per pound. However, keep in mind that from that one pound of snow peas you purchased, you cook and serve at least 95 percent of them. We never get that much yield from English peas. When purchasing snow peas select peas no longer than three inches since peas longer than that have a tendency to be stringy. Also choose peas that are light green in color and firm to the touch. Never take peas that show a yellowish color and have dry ends, for they are past their peak and just do not have the sweetness of young tender peas.

Chinese Squash (*mo qua*). I hate to say it but I have yet to acquire a taste for this vegetable. Maybe it is because of the fuzzy skin. They are light green in color and resemble zucchini, except that they have fuzzy skin and are about six inches long.

Daikon (*low bok*). This giant white radish is about twice the size of a large carrot. Japan is the country that truly loves this vegetable. In fact, it is the number one crop in Japan, where it is very rare to be served a rice dish without daikon. The texture and taste are similar to red radish, but not quite as hot.

Ginger Root—most consumers don't think of it as Oriental, but it is. This brown-skinned beauty has worked its way into many American kitchens, and flavor is the reason. The dry powdered and crystal forms of ginger found in the grocery section of the supermarket just can't stand up when compared to fresh ginger. Fresh ginger is imported from many tropical zones, including the Fiji islands, but the best comes from Hawaii. It is available year round and when stored properly will last for weeks in the refrigerator wrapped tightly in plastic or paper bags. Fresh ginger is extremely versatile and easy to work with. Peel it first, then add very thin slices to salads or use them in a stir fry or with just about any marinade. Next time you are at a supermarket and need ginger, try the fresh stuff first.

Tofu. This item may not be as popular as snow peas or bean sprouts, but it is just as famous and maybe more so. Tofu is the perfect food, some say, and an excellent meat substitute for vegetarians, being extremely high in protein. Tofu is not really a vegetable; rather, it is a byproduct of ground soybeans that have been soaked and allowed to transform into a semisolid mass, then pressed to remove excess moisture. When the process is finished, it looks very much like cheese, and in fact it should be stored in the same manner. I'm not the biggest tofu fan, but I do enjoy it when cooked into Chinese foods or other Oriental dishes.

Wintermelon (*dong qua*). On first sight one might mistake it for a little watermelon, but the resemblance is only in appearance. Inside the flesh is solid white and not sweet at all. Wintermelons are extremely tasty, though, when cooked into fish or shrimp dishes.

Parsnips

Like many old European vegetables, this one was brought to America by the early settlers. It looks just like its relative the carrot, with one exception, color: parsnips are off-white. The parsnip is believed to have originated in the Mediterranean region. By the mid-sixteenth century, this vegetable had established itself as quite an important cash crop throughout Germany, or should I say a survival crop for the poor and underprivileged of that time.

I guess I should tell you that the parsnip is not one of my favorite vegetables, but I do enjoy it on occasion, for a change, especially if the vegetable has been left in the ground until after at least one cold spell. Cold weather allows the starch in this rather bitter vegetable to convert to sugar, which makes it pleasantly sweet (not as sweet as a carrot) and nutty. Therefore I find parsnips best from October through February.

When selecting parsnips, choose small to medium vegetables that are free from scars and damage. If stored properly parsnips will keep in your refrigerator up to seven days in a paper bag. This vegetable contains small amounts of vitamin A. It also contains vitamin C and various other minerals. Since parsnips are related to carrots, they may be substituted in recipes that call for carrots.

Peppers

Peppers, like their botanical cousins, tomatoes, are native to the New World. However, after Columbus introduced them to Europe, the vegetable became popular on that continent, and also rapidly spread throughout the Far East. In fact, hot peppers are cultivated and consumed in such large quantities in India that they are often believed to have originated there.

There are far too many pepper varieties to list them all, but basically there are only two types—*hot* and *sweet.* How do you tell the two apart? You could bite into them, but you may pay the price with a red tongue, so remember this: the bigger the pepper, the milder or sweeter the taste; the smaller the pepper, the hotter the pop.

Two of the hot peppers, also known as chiles, are the *Anahein,* which is considered the mildest of the hot peppers, and the *Pasilla*—also called Poblano or Ancho—which has greenish-black skin and is heart-shaped.

Now for the hot-hot chiles: First is the *Fresno,* which is light green in color, is about one to two inches long, and has a rather pointed end. Next is one of the world's most popular peppers, the *jalapeno,* which is dark green in color and has somewhat of a round cylinder shape. The hottest of all chiles is the *Serrano;* the best way to describe it would be to say it is a miniature jalapeno, but hotter. The Serrano will light you up!

Among the sweet peppers, the most popular are the *bells, green* and *red;* they are the same variety of pepper, but the red ones have been left on the vine long enough to reach full maturity. As green bell pepper ripens the color changes and the flavor becomes sweeter. There are also *yellow, orange,* and *purple bells,* which all start as green. If you would like to try other sweet peppers and break way from the bell, I recommend *Cubanelles,* also known in the South as banana peppers or Italian frying peppers. They are excellent when sautéed with other vegetables.

As for nutrition, all the varieties are great sources of vitamin C and are low in calories. The red bell peppers are also a good source of vitamin A as well as C.

Fresh peppers are available year round, with the season peaking August through September. When shopping, choose peppers high in color and free of bruises, scars, and wrinkles. All are signs of age. Uncut fresh peppers will store in the refrigerator about seven days placed in a paper bag. Once cut, they should be used within three days for best flavor.

Potatoes

Most people think potatoes originated in Ireland, but the potato actually got its start in South America and was brought to Europe by Spanish explorers. In the eighteenth century, settlers from Ireland brought potatoes to North America, so this vegetable became known as *Irish* potatoes. The potato is the world's largest selling fresh vegetable. There is only one crop of potatoes per year, but they are harvested three out of the four seasons. Therefore, the supply is uninterrupted year round. The potatoes dug in fall are usually put in storage. These are best for frying, mashing, and baking, because they don't con-tain as much moisture as fresh potatoes that are dug in spring and summer. In the produce business, potatoes harvested in fall are referred to as "old" potatoes.

"New potatoes" most people think of as red-skinned pota-toes, but new potatoes can be white or red. Potatoes harvested in spring and summer and sold then are new potatoes. Fresh potatoes, because of the moisture, don't fry well, and take a

very long time to bake, but when boiled, they are fantastic.

All red-skinned potatoes are not new potatoes. In the Dakotas and parts of Minnesota, they grow a potato called **Red Bliss.** This potato is harvested in the fall, and put into storage. Most of the Red Bliss potatoes, by the time they are ready to ship to market, have dried out and have been colored with food coloring to enhance their appearance. Most shoppers mistake these for new potatoes. So remember, the Red Bliss potato you see in wintertime is an old potato, so you would save a lot of money if you went ahead and bought the white-skinned potato during winter. For the record, new potatoes that are grown in Florida, California, Arizona, and Texas start to come to market in February. But to be sure the potatoes you are buying are new potatoes, ask your produce person.

Potatoes come in two different shapes: round, which grows mainly east of the Mississippi, and long, grown in the west. First, in California, they grow clear-skinned potatoes named **White Rose;** this is a new potato, but these large white potatoes make good bakers. The other potato grown out west has a brown-colored skin named russett; this potato grows very well in northern California, Oregon, and Washington. When you put the name Idaho in front of a potato, most people think it's a totally different potato, but it's still a **Russet.** The Russet potato is the nation's largest-selling potato; in Idaho they do seem to grow bigger and cleaner. The Russets grown in Idaho also seem to cook better than Russets grown in other areas.

What is the best potato? No, it's not the Russet. The **Finnish** potatoes I think are by far the best all purpose potatoes available. The flesh is yellow, they look fantastic and taste wonderful. When I bake this potato, I don't use butter of salt—just the natural flavor is enough. This type of potato is relatively new in the market place, so please look for it. I'm sure you'll grow to love it as much as I do. Remember, it's Finnish potatoes.

Potatoes are rich in potassium, and vitamin C if unpeeled, naturally low in sodium and fat. One large potato contains about 135 calories. Choose potatoes that are clean and smooth and very firm. Always store potatoes in a cool, dry area with good air circulation.

Rhubarb

In some parts of the country this vegetable (yes, rhubarb is a vegetable, although most people think it is a fruit because of its use in dessert) is known as pie plant.

The rhubarb has quite the medical history. In Colonial days the rhubarb was thought to be a cure for tired blood, and in its homeland of China in ancient times was used primarily for its healing values. Nowadays the only thing it heals is a sweet tooth.

There are two types of rhubarb available for retail consumption: *field grown* and *hot house* ("cultivated" as the producers like to say). The season for field grown begins in spring, and winds down in the fall. In this crop the stalks are most times more green than red, with very large green leaves. The texture is coarse and quite stringy. As for flavor, it is very tart and requires lots of sugar in preparation.

The hot house type begins its season in January and ends in mid-summer; California and Michigan are among the leading suppliers. The color is like that of a nice rosé wine, almost pink, with leaves that are sometimes bright yellow and quite pleasant to the eye. The texture is much less coarse and stringy compared to its outdoor counterpart, as well as tartness in the flavor, therefore requiring much less sugar during preparation.

Rhubarb is available year round, although supplies are limited during November and December. When shopping, choose firm, erect stalks. If leaves are attached, avoid any where there is wilting or dark spots. This vegetable is extremely perishable, so it should be used as soon as possible. If you have to store it, store it refrigerated in a paper bag.

Rhubarb is very high in potassium. A good source for calcium and phosphorus, it also provides some vitamins A and C.

Scallions

Let's clear up two misconceptions at the outset. First, *scallions* and *green onions* are not different types of onions; they are one and the same. Second, no, this thick, grassy-looking vegetable is not a miniature variety of onion. Scallions are young onion plants of any variety that have been harvested before reaching full maturity, usually before the white bulbs reach half an inch in diameter.

Whether you call them scallions or green onions depends on which part of the country you are from. Below the Mason-Dixon Line and to the west Texas state line they're called green onions, except in New Orleans; of course, those Cajuns and Creoles love French-sounding names.

According to most experts the best are grown in California, New Jersey, or the Ohio Valley. To that I say, "What do they have against the South?" I have eaten scallion from New Jersey, Ohio, and California, which all produced excellent crops, and California does lead the nation in production of this little vegetable, but in my opinion, the best come from Georgia. Presently, down in South Georgia, farmers have started to harvest Vidalia green onions during spring, and everyone knows how good Vidalias are.

When you shop for scallions (green onions) let appearance be the judge. If the tops are nice and green and the bottoms are white and clean, you've got a winner. Also keep in mind that 99 percent of this vegetable is edible. We Americans usually disregard those delightful green tops. If you fall into that group, stop; the tops add fantastic flavors to just about anything. When cooking rice or steaming other vegetables, add chopped scallions for a new twist. Add them to beef stew or fried pork chops and chicken, and don't forget scallions are wonderful for garnishing soups and salads.

This little vegetable may not be the most nutritious item in the produce section, but it does contain fair amounts of protein, carbohydrates, and calcium. They are available year round, selling for quite moderate prices.

Shallots

Shallots may very well be the most interesting type of onion, for this little beauty takes characteristics from every member of the onion family. The size is about the same as that of the little green scallion, yet the skin color is a rusty brown, like that of the fully matured Spanish onion. Lastly, the shallot is divided into cloves like its other cousin, garlic. As for flavor, it's not as pungent as garlic, but it adds more zest than the normal Spanish onion we are accustomed to.

The shallot was first introduced to the United States during the middle of the sixteenth century by the French explorer de Soto. This vegetable was very popular in the Louisiana Territory, and it still is in that part of the country. Shallots once were a major cash crop for Louisiana, which produced well in excess of ten million pounds annually. Unfortunately for Louisiana farmers, as the less expensive scallion gained in popularity, shallot sales dropped nearly to nothing. Today, with the advent of gourmet cooking, shallots, which at times bring prices ten times greater than scallions, are making a significant comeback. There are some commercial growers in California, New York, and other parts of the United States, including Louisiana. However, the majority of fresh shallots available to American consumers is imported from Europe, with France being the biggest and best supplier of this gourmet item.

Shallots are available pretty much year round, although new crops of fresh shallots are available July through October. During other months, they come from storage. As for which is best, fresh or seasoned, many professional chefs swear there are no onions as flavorful as fresh shallots, but an equal number of chefs claim shallots need to be seasoned to reach their peak flavor. I have no personal preference.

When shopping, choose shallots less than one inch in diameter unless they are specified as jumbo, which of course are much larger. Although they are easier to handle and work with, jumbo shallots just don't have the flavor of the smaller type. The shallots should be firm, and the skin should be smooth and dry. Avoid shallots in which sprouting has occurred, for sprouting is a sure sign of age and/or improper storage. At home, if stored properly—closed tightly in a brown paper bag and placed in a cool, dark location—shallots will keep for weeks.

As for nutrition, like other members of the onion family, shallots contain fair amounts of vitamins A and C. However, I don't think nutrition is as important with this vegetable because of its size. I don't think anyone would want to eat a half pound of shallots! But I do want to reemphasize the excellent flavor it adds. When your next recipe calls for onion and/or garlic, add diced shallots also. I'm sure you will love the new twist.

Squash

Summer Squash

Zucchini, yellow, and the *white patty pan* are all members of the group that for centuries has been called summer squash. These vegetables are native to the Americas, so by the time the first European settlers arrived, the squash was well established. In fact, "askootasquash" was a staple for the Native Americans. The settlers dropped the first part of the Indian word to come up with the term "squash."

In the past, these squash were available only during the warmer months of the year, and since the season peaks during summer, were labeled "summer" squash. Today with the improved varieties, better agricultural techniques, and refrigeration, zucchini, yellow, and patty pan are in season year round, so the name summer squash may be obsolete.

This group is normally harvested before reaching full maturity, leaving the vegetables with soft, edible shells and seeds. The flesh texture is smooth, creamy, and string-free when cooked, unlike their winter counterparts. The unopened flower of these squash is quite the gourmet item, and sometimes brings as much as fourteen dollars per pound. These squash are very tasty when dipped in egg with salt and pepper, then lightly floured and sautéed.

When shopping for summer squash, freshness is most important; if fresh, the vegetable tends to be on the sweet side; if old, it becomes bitter. Size is also important; for best flavor, choose squash no more than six inches long and two inches wide—both with zucchini and yellow squash. The patty pan should be no more than three to four inches around and one and a half inches high. The squash should be firm, but not hard. Soft squash is old and should be avoided. Squash will store up to a week in the refrigerator.

Summer squash, like its winter cousins, are very nutritious, high in several vitamins: A, B, and C, and also in protein; yet they are low in calories. The mineral value is also good; squash contains fair amounts of calcium and phosphorus and is very high in potassium.

Winter Squash

Acorn squash is also called table queen or Danish squash. It looks like an acorn nut that has large grooves, but it's about the size of a cantaloupe. Its outer skin is very hard and dark green in color with patches of orange.

In these days of hybrid fruits and vegetables, we have been able to grow bigger crops that look fantastic and can be shipped around the world and not be damaged. Sometimes it seems that the growers forgot the most important thing, "taste." The acorn and the other varieties of winter squash are as flavorable today as they were one hundred years ago.

Acorn squash looks good as a table decoration and has a sweet, nutty flavor and a fibrous texture. It can be baked or steamed. *Butternut* squash, another winter variety, does not have as nutty a flavor as acorn, but has a smooth and creamy texture. It can be baked like a sweet potato, but the most common cooking method to boil and mash it.

Other winter squash you may want to try include *Banana* squash, which when fully mature can weigh as much as seventy pounds. Most retailers sell this squash by the slice. *Sweet dumpling* squash looks like a miniature pumpkin and has a large seed cavity which makes it great for stuffing.

Winter squash may be the easiest squash of all to buy. All winter squash has a very hard rind, so hard that at least once a year in the produce business, we hear of someone being hurt by being hit with one of these squash. Therefore hardness is your key. If the squash you select has any soft spots avoid that one and pick another, and if you are buying a slice of squash such as Banana or Hubert squash ask your produce person when the squash was cut to be sure that it has not dried out.

To cook acorn squash, cut in half. Remember to be very careful, since this squash has a very hard rind and your knife may slip. Discard seeds—some winter squash seeds may be roasted and eaten. After squash is halved, sprinkle with brown sugar and butter, then bake 40-45 minutes.

You can also take those two halves and stuff them with meat or sausage and bake it that way. Or try acorn and butternut squash stuffed with ground turkey, mushrooms, and olives, and diced onions.

Winter squash are available starting in autumn and wind down in spring. They are some of the most nutritious vegetables of all; they are loaded with potassium, calcium, and phosphorus and extremely high in vitamin A.

Pumpkins

Pumpkins have been grown in North America for centuries; to the American Indian, the pumpkin was very important. As food, this vegetable (which is a type of winter squash) was harvested in late autumn and would keep well into winter, when meat and other game were scarce. The Indians also used the pumpkin as pottery.

Nowadays the pumpkin is used primarily as an ornamental item. Over 75 percent of all the pumpkins sold in America each year are purchased in the month of October.

When I lived out west, every year I would go to the town of Half Moon Bay, located about sixty miles south of San Francisco, to their annual Pumpkin Festival. It was not uncommon to see pumpkins weighing over two hundred pounds.

Poor pumpkins, on November 1, no one cares about them, because during the month of October, we are all in search of that perfect, orange spiral-shaped winter squash to transform into "Mr. Jack-O'-Lantern."

Remember, after carving that Jack-O'-Lantern, the pumpkin seeds make good snacks after being roasted. Simply wash them and pat dry, then salt and place a little butter on the roasting pan and bake at 400 degrees about 15 minutes.

For people in the produce business, pumpkins are the true sign of autumn. They start to show up on the market in late August. By the end of September, from the Golden Gate Produce Terminal in San Francisco to Hunts Point Market in New York, the world of fresh vegetables is overrun by the largest and one of the tastiest of the winter squash. By November 1, they are all but gone.

When shopping for pumpkins, be it for Jack-O'-Lanterns or for making fresh pies, choose vegetables with fresh green stems, that are free of scars or soft spots. That pumpkin will keep for weeks on your front porch.

Like the other winter squash, the pumpkin is extremely nutritious and low in calories. It is very high in vitamin A, calcium, and potassium.

Sweet Potatoes and Yams

Here in the United States, the terms sweet potato and yams are used interchangeably, but the two are different. Sweet potatoes are the swollen roots of a vine related to the morning glory family. I think the best-tasting ones are grown in the South. Yams, on the other hand, are actually native to the tropics and are rarely available fresh in the local grocery store.

Sweet potatoes originated in Central America, but now are grown in every subtropical climate on earth. The Portuguese took sweet potatoes to India and Malaya and the Spaniards, to the Indies. They even tried to introduce sweet potatoes to Europe, however the climate is just too cool for their cultivation. In fact, to this day, when compared to its worldwide popularity in Europe, sweet potatoes are virtually unknown. In

Asia, sweet potatoes are so popular they are often referred to as Japanese potatoes.

There are basically two types of sweet potatoes grown in the United States. The one most people call yams has orange-colored flesh. Over the past eight years a red-fleshed sweet potato has increased in popularity; North Carolina and Louisiana are among the leading producing states of these each year. These potatoes, when fresh, are moist and very sweet. The other sweet potato has a pale-yellow or whitish flesh color. They are often called Jersey sweet; they are not quite as sweet as the deeper colored potatoes, but they are still very tasty.

Sweet potatoes are available year round with a peak season August through September. When shopping, remember: small to medium sweet potatoes usually have a better flavor and smoother texture. Choose firm, uniform potatoes that are free of cuts and scars. Also avoid any potato with wet spots or mold. **Sweet potatoes should never be stored in the refrigerator.** Always store in a cool dry area. They will keep up to two weeks, but try to consume them sooner.

Sweet potatoes are one of our most versatile and nutritious vegetables. In fact, in many undeveloped countries, this vegetable is used as the major food staple. One medium sweet potato contains about twice the daily requirement of vitamin A and has only about 130 calories. They are also high in vitamin C and contain large amounts of iron. You can bake them, fry them, and do something else you probably have never tried— sweet potatoes are great raw in tossed salad.

Tomatoes

The tomato is technically a vegetable; in fact, it is the third most popular vegetable, ranking behind lettuce and potatoes. As popular as tomatoes are, you would think we Americans have been eating them since we stepped off the *Mayflower*. (Well, I'm sure my ancestors did not step off the *Mayflower*, but you know what I mean.) Not so. Tomatoes belong to the nightshade family which includes some deadly fruits. For that reason, the early settlers were afraid to consume this item. Well, they finally started to eat them around 1880, and tomatoes soon became a strong cash crop, which they still are. That is when the question "is it a fruit or a vegetable?" came up for the first time because of trade regulations pertaining to the two different groups. Around 1893, the United States Supreme Court ruled that tomatoes are a vegetable.

For the last few years, different colors and shapes of tomatoes have been making quite an impact on our market: pink, orange, pear-shaped, cherry tomatoes, and yellow ones, to name a few. I can still remember the first time I ate a yellow pear tomato. I was in a restaurant in Los Angeles, and my eyes almost jumped out of my head. The taste was wonderful. I grabbed a handful and brought them out of the restaurant with me. When I got back to San Francisco, I bragged on the pretty yellow tomatoes I had eaten. Charlie Benicort, one of the most knowledgeable men in the United States on exotic produce, said to me, "Curtis, the first tomatoes grown were yellow," which was quite a surprise to me. Now, the next time you are in one of those fancy gourmet stores—you know, like the one I dream of owning some day—and see an advertisement for new pear-shaped or yellow tomatoes, you'll know there is nothing new about them. It's just that we have rediscovered them.

When shopping for tomatoes (of any variety or shape), look for full-colored, ripe but firm vegetables that are free of bruises. By "full color," I mean red all over or, if you are buying orange tomatoes, orange from the blossom (top) end to the stem (bottom) end where the vegetable was removed from the plant. If you want to prepare one of our southern favorites, fried green tomatoes, then it's OK to buy green tomatoes. Otherwise, green or immature tomatoes just don't reach that peak flavor.

Avoid soft, spongy tomatoes for sandwiches and salads. However, those tomatoes should not be thrown out, for they are perfect for cooking in soups or sauces.

Firm tomatoes will keep unrefrigerated for about two, maybe three days before you notice them becoming softer. At that point it is OK to refrigerate them. If you or your family don't consume them within two additional days, freeze them, for they will cook just as well in six months.

As for the nutritional content of tomatoes, they are loaded! They're packed with calcium, phosphorus, and potassium—not to mention vitamin A. All of that, and only about twenty-five calories per medium tomato!

HERBS

HERBS

In Latin the word *herba* means "grass." *The American Heritage Dictonary* defines *herb* as "(1) plant that has a fleshy stem as distinguished from the woody tissue of shrubs and trees, and that dies back at the end of each growing season." This is an excellent botanical definition, but the definition we greengrocers think of is "(2) any of various often aromatic plants used especially in medicine or as seasoning." This definition almost gives a history of the plant group.

Through the ages herbs, fresh or dried, have been prized for their aromatic value; I wouldn't be surprised if they were first used by some caveperson as an air freshener.

Herbs have also been praised for their healing powers. They have been used in medicine for thousands of years, but they have also been feared for their connection with the supernatural. If you don't believe me, check out the voodoo shops in New Orleans.

Most of all, through the centuries herbs have been loved for their ability to improve the flavor of foods they are added to. During the Middle Ages and before refrigeration, herbs were used very heavily to cover the smell and foul taste of old meat, meat that by today's standards would be considered rotten. With better storage and cooking facilities we've found that less herbs means better taste.

In this section I will discuss some of the most common herbs and would like to see people make more use of them. Buy only herbs with fresh stems and leaves, in small quantities.

Anise

Like its relative fennel, anise has a licorice flavor. It cooks well with root vegetables and adds a nice touch when seasoning chicken or fish. Be careful not to overseason, for a little goes a long way. That is a good rule to remember when using all herbs, fresh or dry.

Basil

This fresh-smelling, sweet-flavored herb is a staple in most Italian kitchens, and it's also believed to be a money charm. The Italian guys I worked with at Balducci's in New York—Gino, Sal, and Mario—all told me that if you keep a fresh basil leaf in your wallet you'll always have money. Every morning those guys would take out the old leaf and replace it with a fresh one. Never worked for me.

Basil is available year round. During cold months it's grown in hothouses and is sold in small bunches. The quality is excellent, but it can be quite expensive. During the warm seasons field basil is available; this is the time to make loads of pesto and freeze it for winter. Field basil is about ten times larger than the hothouse type and less than half the price.

This herb is one of the most perishable items in the produce section; therefore, it should be used as soon as possible. If you have to store it, when you get home wrap the basil in a wet paper towel, then place it in a plastic bag and refrigerate. It may keep two or three days.

In addition to common basil, over the past few years *red basil* (in the big cities it's called "opal basil") has made an impression on the gourmet scene. It should be selected and stored in the same manner as green basil. Try these two fresh basil recipes:

BAKED TOMATO:

With a paring knife cut a hole in the tomato, pull whole section out, set aside, chop 2 or 3 basil leaves and half a clove of garlic, stuff inside of tomato with a bit of margarine and salt and pepper, cover the hole with the cut-out part and bake in 375 degree oven about 30 minutes.
Serve on a bed of rice.

PESTO: THE ITALIAN CLASSIC:

Ingredients:
> 1 cup chopped basil
> 2 cloves garlic, chopped
> 1/2 oz. chopped parsley

Instructions:
> Mix ingredients well, add 1/4 cup olive oil, and serve. You can also add Parmesan cheese.

Chives

Remember earlier I said that in Latin *herba* means "grass"? Well, the person that wrote that definition must have been eating chives at the time, because this native to Eurasia has green, grass-like hollow leaves, and when they're young, you can't tell the difference.

Although I'm covering chives in the herb section, and although most people in the produce business think of them as an herb, they're not. In truth chives are a member of the onion family, the unusual member. This is strange in two ways: first, they are so tiny, and, second, the only usable part is the green, grassy top. They have a mild onion flavor and mix very well with the other food groups; chives and creamed cheese makes a delightful spread, chives and cottage cheese also tastes great, chives are delicious added to baked potatoes, and the next time you roast a chicken, season it as you usually do, but add about one ounce of finely chopped chives.

Chives come in small bunches and are available year round. When shopping for them, avoid yellow or slimy leaves. When you get them home, I recommend using them as soon as possible, for the longer they sit, the more flavor is lost. If you have to store chives, place them in a paper bag, then put the bag in a dry place in your refrigerator. Sometimes you can find planted pots of chives in your produce market. I'm no farmer, but even I can take care of potted chives. You just water them and put them back in the windowsill. The great thing is that you can cut off what you need whenever you want fresh chives, and they grow back.

Cilantro

There are about forty members of the parsley family, and cilantro is one; in fact, it has the strongest flavor and smell of all the parsleys, though to look at it you wouldn't think so. The leaves are flat and somewhat delicate in appearance and not as colorful as other parsleys. However, all that changes when you bring it to your nose. That strong smell grabs you, but it's not overpowering—instead it's refreshing and clean. The taste is the same—very refreshing.

Cilantro is also known as coriander and as Chinese parsley. I guess by the names you can tell that this herb is used quite often in Latin, Hispanic, and Oriental dishes. However, this herb is surely cutting into main stream American cuisine. Try adding fresh cilantro to salads with a light dressing. Use it to season beans, meats, and vegetables.

Dill

Today this herb is most often thought of in conjunction with pickles. However, over the centuries dill has been used for many purposes, from cooking to medicine, and even as a deterrent for witches. Its exact origin is unclear, but dill was written about by the early Egyptians some five thousand years ago. The name "dill" comes from the Norwegian word *dilla* ("soothe" or "lull"). The ground herb was fed to babies to sooth their stomachs and lull them to sleep. Fresh dill is still one of nature's best laxatives. At one time it was believed that hanging fresh dill over the doorway would protect the home from witches and other evils. One of the commercial uses for dill is in scenting soaps. However, we care more for its culinary value, right?

Dill can add a new zip to any vegetable dish as well as livening up simple salads. When shopping, avoid dill that has started to yellow and choose dill high in color with a strong aroma; lack of smell is a sign of age, but that is OK if you plan to dry them. The next time you make potato salad, add dill, and for an easy sauce excellent with salmon and trout, melt butter or margarine over high heat; while still hot, add fresh chopped dill, then pour over fish.

Marjoram

Now this is an interesting plant. Marjoram is a member of the mint family, and on close inspection of the oval, gray-green leaves and the minty aroma, you can notice the resemblance. Another member of the mint family is oregano (see below), which means that marjoram is a great substitute for oregano, and vice versa. The two plants are very similar in appearance and aroma, although marjoram is not quite as pungent, which may explain why it's not called for as often in Italian recipes as its cousin. Herbalists credit marjoram with being an excellent remedy for stomach disorders. In cooking, this herb is at its seasoning best when combined with thyme. Marjoram is wonderful when added to meats, fish, vegetables, and stuffing for poultry.

Oregano

The name comes from two Greek words—*oros*, meaning "mountain" and *ganos*, meaning "joy." Centuries ago oregano and its other family members, marjoram and wild marjoram, filled the hills of the Mediterranean areas with their beautiful purple flowers and became a symbol of happiness. In Greece if the plants were found growing on or near a gravesite, that was believed to be a sign that the person buried there was very happy.

During medieval times an extract from oregano was used to relieve pain from toothache. This herb is not as rich in color as other fresh herbs, which may be why oregano has a much longer shelf life. With its strong flavor and aroma oregano truly livens up dishes it is added to. It's great on pizza or with baked tomatoes or any tomato-based dish.

Parsley

This is the most common herb, but most people don't even think of eating parsley. We think of it as that green stuff that has no purpose and is always on your plate in restaurants. Originally, parsley was put on plates as an after-meal breath freshener; try eating it next time and notice how clean your mouth and breath feel.

There are nearly forty types of parsley, but here in the South we usually only have one variety available to us: the Neapolitan, or curly parsley. Now up north and out west the shopper fares a little better. They have two varieties: the curly kind and the flat, broad-leafed Italian parsley.

This cousin of the carrot originated in the Mediterranean area and outside of the United States it's as popular as it is common, not only as garnish but also in cooked dishes and as a base green for a salad. To make a sauce good with meat or vegetables and simply excellent over potatoes, sautée chopped parsley in margarine and oil (olive or vegetable); for a little more zap add chopped onions or shallots.

Before I give you a salad recipe I want you to know how nutritious this herb is. If consumed in larger amounts (three to five ounces) parsley supplies more vitamin A than carrots, more vitamin C than oranges, and about one third the potassium of a banana. It's also high in calcium, phosphorus, and riboflavin—and low in calories. So with that in mind, eat more parsley.

Parsley Salad:

Ingredients:

   3 cups parsley leaf cleaned and stemmed
   5 tomatoes chopped
   1 cup cracked wheat
   1 bunch chopped green onions
   1/3 cup fresh lemon juice
   1/3 cup virgin olive oil
   1 tbs. pepper
   1 oz. fresh mint, chopped

Instructions:

   At least 12 hours before serving mix together tomatoes, wheat, onions, juice, pepper, and mint. Refrigerate. 30 min. before serving add parsley and oil. Serve on romaine leaf.

Once you get the parsley home, plunge the fresh herb into cold water (this extends the storage life), place in a paper bag, and store in the refrigerator. It should keep five days.

Rosemary

This is the symbol of remembrance; in ancient Greece students wore fresh rosemary in their hair because it was believed to sharpen their memory. During marriage ceremonies, Greek women wore the herb to indicate that they would never forget their families, and the dead were laid to rest with rosemary so they would always be remembered.

Rosemary's culinary values are endless. The ancient cooks discovered this, using rosemary to help tame the tastes of wild meats—rabbit and deer, as well as poultry. Today rosemary is a "must" on herb racks and in fresh herb gardens. It is still used primarily to season meat and fish or poultry, but I want to point out that it seasons fresh vegetables very well. Try adding rosemary next time you steam veggies, and it's also great with boiled potatoes.

Sage

On first sight you may wonder if it's vegetable or animal because of its fuzzy, silver leaves. In gourmet kitchens sage is called the perfect poultry seasoning. Its flavor has been described as musty, which is pretty accurate. Try adding fresh ground sage to your next roasted chicken, but don't stop with poultry, for this herb adds something special when seasoning fish or meats (especially beef or pork). Fresh sage should be stored in a tightly sealed paper bag, then refrigerated. It should keep three or four days.

Tarragon

You could call this one the French herb, for its slightly licorice flavor is found in many French dishes. Tarragon is to my eye the prettiest of the fresh herbs, with its slender green leaves that bring to mind palm leaves. One of the classic uses for

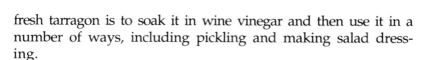

fresh tarragon is to soak it in wine vinegar and then use it in a number of ways, including pickling and making salad dressing.

PICKLED MELONS:

Ingredients:
    1/2 cup tarragon wine vinegar
    1 tbs. finely chopped fresh dill and mint
    2 to 3 cups assorted melons cut into 1-inch squares

Instructions:
    In large bowl combine all ingredients, cover, and chill three to four hours before serving.

Thyme

This is another favorite of the French, though the Creoles of Lousiana are the real thyme keepers. You can taste thyme in almost every Creole dish, from fish to chicken and from beef to vegetables. Some describe the smell as pungent, and I think its aroma is heavenly fresh, dried, and while being cooked. The flavor is spicy but not hot. There is also lemon thyme available; it is a wonderful natural blend of thyme with the lemon flavor and aroma, excellent with seafoods. Try serving this **sauce** over your favorite seafood dish: *1 oz. fresh lemon thyme chopped fine and 1 oz. fresh dill, chopped, sautéed in margarine with about 3 oz. cream.*

NUTS

NUTS

The overall health benefit of eating nuts is that they are excellent body builders, great sources for fat, carbohydrates, calcium, protein, and many other nutrients the body needs in development.

Almonds

There are two kinds of almonds, sweet and bitter. The bitter almond is never sold as a table fruit. It is purchased by processors that transform its oil into flavorings and extracts. The sweet almond is the one you will find in your produce section. This one can be subdivided into two groups: soft shell and hard shell. The soft shells are much easier to open, but carry a higher price tag. I think for the extra time in cracking the hard shell you not only save money, but also get a much better tasting nut.

California is the world's largest producer of this native to the Mediterranean basin. Almonds are available year round with very few swings in price.

Brazil Nuts

I loved those nuts as a kid, but they are so hard to crack. If you saw a Brazil nut fresh from the tree, you might mistake it for a coconut. They look so much alike. That is where the similarities end though, because beneath the shell, instead of liquid, you will find about twenty tightly-fitting segments. These are the Brazil nuts you are used to finding in the produce section. Although Brazil nuts have a very hard shell and hard meat, the nut will spoil if not stored properly in a cool, dry area.

Cashews

Another South American native nut is the cashew. Nowadays, the majority of the cashews we consume come from India. Believe it or not, this nut is related to one of my favorite tropical fruits—mangoes. With the mango, you eat the meat and throw away the seed. Cashews are reversed—discard the flesh or meat, and roast and enjoy the seed. In the supermarket you will find shelled and roasted, sometimes raw, cashews.

Chestnuts

In most of the gourmet shops, you will find chestnuts imported from Italy, and not because that's the best chestnut of all time. Around the turn of the century, three types of chestnuts were found: Oriental, European, and American. The American chestnut is believed to have been the best chestnut of all. Unfortunately, during that same period of time, a chestnut blight totally wiped out the entire American crop.

Chestnuts are usually priced according to size. They are medium, large, and extra large or jumbo. Different areas of the country use different labels to determine size. Normally, the larger the size, the higher the price. I can't determine a big enough difference in taste from large to small to pay the difference in price, so my recommendation is for the less expensive ones. Most of us know of roasting chestnuts, but here is a *French dessert topping* you may want to give a try during the holiday season: Take chestnut meat and boil it in sugar syrup with vanilla flavoring. It's scrumptious.

Hazel nuts

My appreciation for this nut didn't develop until my first trip to Europe. Being a Southerner, I was much more familiar with pecans, peanuts, and black walnuts, so during the holiday season I always picked over the smooth, hard-shelled round brown things that reminded me of large acorns. In Europe, though, the hazel nut (also called filberts because the first day of harvest is August 22— St. Filbert's Day) is everywhere. It is used as a table food, is great in baking, and mixes well with chocolate. In fact, I first tasted this nut in a candy bar in Paris. I asked my companion what was this fantastic nut, and then went out and bought two kilos to take back to our hotel. Turkey is by far the world's largest producer of the hazel nut; next is Italy, and there is a small crop grown in the western United States.

Macadamia Nuts

These nuts are not native to Hawaii, as many people think. They originated in Australia, then were transplanted to Hawaii, where, along with pineapples, they have become a major export and cash crop for that tropical paradise. Macadamias are one of the most oily and flavorful nuts of all. Unshelled, this nut looks very similar to the hazel nut, except that the macadamia's shell is as hard as a rock. In fact, it takes some 350 pounds of pressure per square inch to crack one, so please never try it with your teeth. The macadamia is high in price and fat, but it is also a good source for protein, calcium, and carbohydrates.

Peanuts

My home state of Georgia may no longer lead the nation in peach production, but it is still number one in peanuts. The peanut is really a member of the legume family, the same as peas and beans, except for one difference: the peanut is developed underground, and so is called "ground nut" in some places. Peanuts are available year round in one form or another. They are also an excellent source for protein.

Pecans

Most years Georgia produces more than half of all the pecans sold in America. In fact, there is only one other nut more popular than our Southern pecan: the walnut. The pecan is native to North America. There are very few, if any, pecan trees in Europe. So if you have friends in Europe, and want to impress them with your gourmet gifts, send pecans or pecan candies.

Pistachios

When I was a kid someone asked if I would like to try pistachio ice cream. I said, "No way." I thought it was some weird flavor like licorice, and I didn't want to have any part of it. I think I had my first pistachio nut at age twenty. It was love at first crack. Iran and Turkey lead world production in this light-green-colored nut, which belongs to the same family as cashews and mangoes. Nowadays, in your produce market, you can find pistachios from California as well. The meat is light green, but the hard shell is almost colorless in its natural tone. Some processors color this nut red before shipping to market. I opt for the natural color if I have a choice. The reason most pistachios are partially cracked is because of that extremely hard shell. The slight crack makes it easier for the consumer to get at the goody.

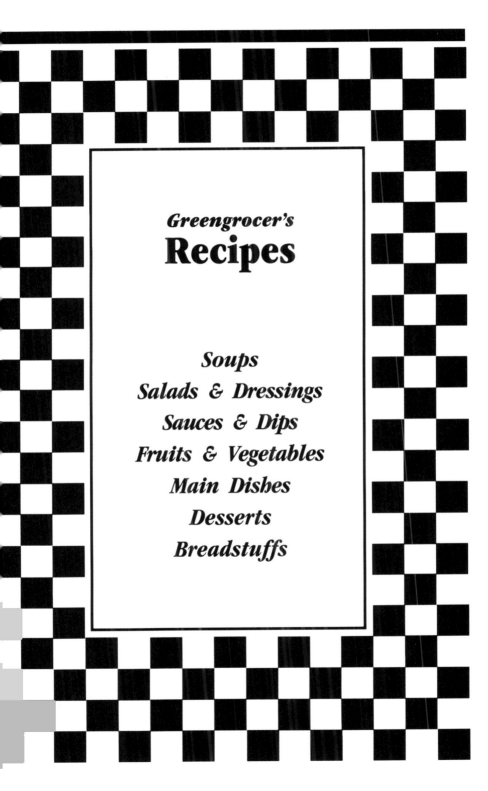

Greengrocer's
Recipes

Soups
Salads & Dressings
Sauces & Dips
Fruits & Vegetables
Main Dishes
Desserts
Breadstuffs

Soups

Curtis's Minestrone

    8 oz. white cannellini beans *(if dry, soak overnight in cold water)*
    3 tbs. olive oil
    1 turkey leg
    1 onion, chopped
    2 cloves garlic, chopped
    4 sticks celery, chopped
    2 carrots, diced
    1 small head savoy or green cabbage
    4 oz. green beans cut into 1-inch pieces
    8 oz. tomatoes, diced
    1 dried red chile
    10 cups water
    1 sprig fresh rosemary
    1 bay leaf
    12 oz. pasta
    3 zucchini, peeled and diced
    1 tbs. each fresh chopped basil and parsley
    salt and pepper

In large pot add oil, turkey leg, onion and garlic; sauté until onions are soft. Add celery, carrots, cabbage, and green beans. Drain beans and add to pot along with tomatoes and chile. Add water and bring to boil. Add rosemary and bay leaf. Simmer uncovered about 1-1/2 hours. Add pasta; cook about 10 min. Add zucchini. Cook about 20 min. more. Remove rosemary and bay leaf. Add herbs, salt and pepper.

Potato Leek Soup

> 3 oz. margarine
> 4 leeks chopped
> 2 stalks celery, chopped
> 1 onion chopped
> 3 large potatoes, chopped
> 1-1/2 qts. water
> 1-1/2 cups cream
> salt and pepper to taste

In a large pot, add margarine, leeks, celery, and onion. Sauté about 8 minutes. Add potatoes and water and bring to boil. Lower heat and simmer about 30 minutes. During last 5 minutes of cooking, add cream and seasoning. *(Don't forget the garlic bread!)*

Cream of Broccoli, Cauliflower, or Celery Soup

Just exchange the vegetables

> 2 cups chopped broccoli
> 2 carrots diced
> 4 tbs. margarine
> 2 cups diced onions
> 3 tbs. flour
> 6 cups hot chicken broth
> salt and pepper to taste
> 1 cup whipping cream

Place 1 cup broccoli and carrots in pan. Add 1 cup broth. Cook until tender, about 4 min. Drain and set aside. In large pot, add margarine. Sauté onions until clear; add flour and cook about 2 min. DO NOT BROWN. Add chicken broth. Whisk well until mixture boils, being sure to reach bottom of pan. Simmer about 30 min. Strain off vegetables and place into blender with 1-1/2 cups liquid, and puree. Stir back into pot with remaining broth. Stir in cream and set aside cooked vegetables. Heat and serve.

Georgia's Onion Soup
(Vidalia when available)

       4 onions
       4 tbs. margarine
       4 cups chicken broth
       1 cup white wine
       salt and pepper to taste
       2 tbs. fresh chopped herbs
       cornbread or muffins
       cheese

In a pot, sauté onions with margarine, until soft. Add broth, wine, seasoning, and herbs. Simmer about 35 min. In serving bowl place a slice of cornbread. Sprinkle with cheese. Add soup and serve.

Jack-O'-Lantern Soup

       1 pumpkin top carved, and inside cleaned
       1/2 lb. cubed sugar pumpkin
       4 tbs. melted margarine
       salt and pepper
       1 cup chopped onion
       1/2 cup each chopped carrots and celery
       4 cup chicken broth
       1 cup tomatoes diced
       1/4 cup rice

Coat inside of pumpkin with half the melted margarine, and sprinkle inside with salt and pepper. Bake in 400 degree oven 20 min. Sauté mixed vetetables in other margarine about 5 min. Add broth. Bring to a boil. Pour broth and vegetables along with rice into pumpkin. Return to oven with lid on top. Bake about 60 min. or until pumpkin is tender, but not too soft. Place whole pumpkin on dinner table.

Melon Soup

    8 lbs. melons (your choice)
    2 tsp. vegetable oil
    2 fresh chili peppers seeded and chopped
    1/2 cup wine
    2/3 cup lemon juice
    2 tbs. honey
    1/4 tsp. pepper

Cut melons, remove seeds, and scoop out flesh—set aside. In sauce pan, heat oil. Cook peppers about 4 min. Add wine and boil. In large bowl, mix melons with hot wine and peppers, add other ingredients. Purée in blender. Chill before serving.

Chicken Soup

One of the dishes I made for Evander Holyfield out in Reno. (Of course you don't have to make this much; I was feeding 7 or 8 huge guys.)

    8 lbs. chicken, cut into bite sized pieces
    2 large onion, chopped
    2 leeks, chopped
    1 bunch celery, chopped
    1 bunch broccoli, chopped
    2 lbs. carrots, chopped
    margarine
    Worcestershire sauce
    salt and pepper
    a bit of sage
    water

In a pot, sauté chicken in margarine and Worcestershire sauce about 4 min. Add about 2 or 3 cups of water. Boil 20 to 30 min. to ensure a thick broth. Add chicken bones during cooking.You can add onion and leeks now. What I do is sauté all the other chopped vegetables about 3 min. in margarine and a dash of salt and pepper before adding to chicken. Then simmer about 40 min. Serve with cornbread.

Ground Turkey Soup

    1 lb. ground turkey
    5 cup water
    4 onions, chopped
    4 carrots, chopped
    4 celery ribs, chopped
    6 tomatoes, diced
    4 potatoes, peeled and diced
    1/2 broccoli, chopped
    salt and pepper to taste
    1 oz. each thyme and sage, chopped
    2 tbs. margarine

In a large pot, sauté turkey with margarine and herbs for about 6 min. Add vegetables and cook 5 min. more. Add water and simmer about 1-1/2 hours.

Vegetarian Chili

    2 tbs. margarine
    1 onion, chopped
    2 cloves garlic, chopped
    1 cups mushrooms, sliced
    1 green pepper, chopped
    4 cups red kidney beans
    8 tomatoes, chopped
    2 tbs. chili powder *(if you like it hot, add chopped jalapeno pepper)*

In a large pot, add margarine, onions, and garlic. Sauté until onions are clear. Add mushrooms and pepper. Cook about 2 min. Add tomatoes, beans, and chili powder. Simmer about 45 min. Season to taste.

French Salad and Dressing

 1 head romaine lettuce, washed and cut
  into bite size pieces
 2 hard boiled eggs, quartered
 6 anchovies, chopped (optional)
 10 pitted black olives
 1/4 cucumber, diced
 1 can tuna, drained
 4 large artichoke hearts, quarted

Dressing:

 1/3 cup olive oil
 2 tbs. white wine
 1/2 clove garlic, chopped
 1 tsp. mustard
 juice of 1/2 lemon

In a large salad bowl add romaine, set aside eggs, add all remaining salad ingredients and toss. Add eggs. Mix together dressing ingredients. Pour over salad, toss again, and serve.

Butter Bean and Tuna Salad

 1 lb. cooked butter beans *(if you can't find fresh, you may use frozen)*
 6 oz. canned tuna
 juice of one lemon
 1 oz. blend of fresh chopped herbs of your choice
 8 tbs. olive oil
 salt and pepper to taste
 6 plum tomatoes sliced

In a shallow serving dish place beans. Add tuna to beans. Mix together lemon juice, herbs, and olive oil. Add to beans. Toss and season with salt and pepper. Surround salad with sliced plum tomatoes and serve.

Curtis's Aloha Pasta Salad

8 to 12 oz. of your favorite pasta noodles, cooked
4 oz. snow peas
2 big broccoli tops *(steam both vegetables about 4 min.)*
1/2 fresh pineapple, diced
1 Vidalia onion, diced
2 celery stalks, diced
1 can white tuna
4 to 6 oz. vinaigrette *(recipe on p. 129, minus the mustard)*

Mix all together. I think the salad is best chilled.

Parsley Salad

3 cups parsley, cleaned and stemmed
5 tomatoes, chopped
1 cup cracked wheat
1 bunch green onion, chopped
1/3 cup lemon juice
1/3 cup olive oil
1 oz. mint, chopped
salt and pepper to taste

At least 24 hours before serving, mix tomatoes, wheat, onions, juice, oil, and seasoning. Refrigerate. 30 min. before serving, add parsley. Mix, then serve.

Quilla's Carrot Salad

4 lbs. sheared carrots
3 tbs. sugar
1 lb. raisins
2 cups diced pineapple
3 tbs. mayonnise

Combine all ingredients; toss and serve. Quilla tells me for best flavor, make the salad a day ahead.

Dandelion Salad with Orange Soy Dressing

Choose 1 pound of dandelion leaves; the smaller and younger the better. Wash and dry carefully. Set aside. In a mixing bowl add 1/2 cup fresh orange juice, 1 tsp. grated orange peel, 2 tbs. soy sauce, 1 tsp. grated fresh ginger, 3 tbs. olive oil, 1 clove of garlic, chopped fine, and salt and pepper to taste. When ready to serve, pour over dandelion greens. Toss.

Spread:

Combine in blender 1 cup young, tender dandelion greens, 1/2 cup cottage cheese, 1 qt. chopped nuts (could be pecans, walnuts, whatever you desire), and your favorite dressing. Add enough dressing to make the mixture the right consistency to spread onto crackers. Makes 1/4 to 3/4 cups spread.

Beets and Pears with Dandelion Greens and Mustard Vinaigrette

Vinaigrette:
    2 tbs. dijon mustard
    2 tbs. finely chopped mild red onions
    2 tbs. distilled white vinegar
    1/3 cup salad oil

Mix all ingredients together.

Other ingredients:
    1 med. pear
    3 cups young tender dandelion greens
    2 med. beets (cooked, peeled, and cut into
        1/8-inch strips)
    1 to 2 tbs. finely chopped nuts (any you like)

Peel and core pear, cut into 1/8-inch strips and immediately mix with vinaigrette to prevent darkening. Arrange dandelion greens evenly on 4 serving plates. Makes 2 or 3 alternating layers of beets and peas on each plate. Pour vinaigrette dressing over your salad. Sprinkle nuts on the top and serve.

Yam Salad

3 large yams, peeled and boiled
1 large sweet onion, sliced thin
1/2 green, yellow, and red peppers, sliced into strips
4 oz. vinaigrette dressing and 2 oz. honey mixed

Mix all ingredients in large bowl. Chill *(overnight for best flavor)* before serving.

Mama's Potato Salad

4 potatoes peeled, diced, and boiled (cool)
3 hard-boiled eggs, chopped (cool)
1 celery rib, diced
1/4 pepper, diced
1 small onion, diced
2 tbs. pimiento
2 tbs. sweet relish
4 tbs. mayonnaise
1 tbs. mustard
1/2 tsp. salt, pepper, and sugar

Combine all ingredients, mixing well. Chill and serve.

Mama's Cole Slaw

1 med. cabbage, grated
1 onion, grated
1 carrot, grated
1 pepper, chopped
2 tbs. sweet relish
1/2 cup mayo
1 tbs. sugar
1/2 tsp. lemon juice
1/2 tsp. vinegar

Mix all ingredients. Chill and serve.

Salad New Orleans
 5 tomatoes diced
 8 sliced zucchini
 1 each red, yellow, and green pepper, chopped
 1 avocado, diced
 1 onion, chopped
 3 green onions, chopped
 2 tsp. sugar
 salt and pepper to taste

Toss all ingredients; let rest to blend flavors, about 1 hour. Chill and serve.

Three Bean Salad
(This is one of the few salads I will use canned vegetables in.)
 3 large cans assorted beans, drained
 1/2 cup sugar
 1/2 cup olive oil
 1/2 each red, yellow, and green pepper, chopped
 1 onion, sliced in rings
 1 oz. each tarragon and basil, chopped
 2 oz. parsley, chopped
 1/2 tsp. dry mustard
 1/2 cup vinegar

Mix all ingredients in large bowl. Chill a day ahead.

Jenny's Herbal Salad Dressing

1 cup oil
1/2 cup white wine vinegar
1 tbs. Dijon mustard
2 tsp. horseradish
2 tsp. sugar
1 oz. fresh chopped tarragon
2-1/2 oz. fresh chopped basil
1/2 onion, chopped
1 tbs. lemon juice
2 tbs. Lawry's seasoning
3/4 tsp. black pepper
2 cloves garlic, chopped

Mix all ingredients together. Serve over your favorite salad. For best flavor, make 24 hours ahead.

Caesar Salad Dressing

2 cloves garlic, chopped
6 tbs. olive oil
4 tbs. lemon juice
2 tbs. Worcestershire sauce
1/2 tsp. pepper
1 soft-boiled egg, mashed
5 tbs. grated Parmesan cheese
8 anchovies, chopped fine

Mix all ingredients well. Serve over romaine and croutons.

Eggplant Salad Dressing
2 eggplant
3 cloves garlic chopped
1/2 cup oil
1/3 cup vinegar
1/3 cup white wine
salt and pepper

Cut eggplant into 1-inch pieces; salt and let drain about 20 min. Pat dry and place in baking pan. Cover with garlic and oil. Bake at 400 degrees (about 15 min.), or until tender and brown. Cool and pour into mixing bowl. Add remaining ingredients. Mix well. Great on salad or potato dishes.

All Apple Salad with Florida Dressing
6 different apples, cored and diced
1 4-oz. container strawberry yogurt
juice from 4 different Florida citruses (*1 Valencia, 1 navel, 1 tangerine, 1 tangelo*)

In a large bowl, place apples. Mix yogurt and juices, and pour over apples. Chill and serve.

Banana Salad Dressing
2 ripe bananas, mashed
1-1/2 tbs. dry mustard
1 cup sour cream
1/2 cup sugar
1 tsp. salt
2 tbs. orange juice

Blend all ingredients together. Chill before using. *For salad or fruits.*

Fresh Pineapple Dressing

    1/2 cup pineapple, chopped
    4 tbs. white wine
    2 tbs. vinegar
    2 cloves garlic, chopped
    1 oz. each fresh basil and marjoram

Mix all ingredients. Serve over salad greens or baked potato.

Sauces & Dips

Three Quick and Easy Fresh Herb Condiments

Raspberry and Herb Vinegar — Any fresh herb is great with vinegar: sage, thyme, basil. The French favorite is tarragon; however, I prefer mint, and will serve it over fruit salad.

To 12 oz. white wine vinegar, add 1 to 2 oz. fresh mint and 1 oz. raspberries. Place bottle in sunny spot for 2 to 3 weeks (shake every other day if you can) before using.

Herb Butter(margarine) — 1 stick butter or margarine, creamed until fluffy. Blend in 1/4 cup fine chopped fresh herbs. Eggs cooked with this butter are great.

To make garlic butter: to a stick of butter, add 1 tbs. minced garlic and 3 tbs. parsley. Place in mold and chill.

Herb Jelly — Empty a 10 oz. jar of apple jelly into a sauce pan. Heat until semi-liquid, then add 1/4 cup finely chopped herbs. Sage with roasted chicken, glazed with herb jelly is fabulous.

Ginger Garlic Dip

      2 oz. fresh ginger, finely chopped
      3 cloves garlic finely, chopped
      1 cup mayonnaise
      1 cup sour cream
      1/4 cup chopped parsley
      1/4 cup water chestnuts
      1-1/2 tbs. soy sauce

Mix all ingredients well. Chill and serve with vegetables.

Mustard Sauce

    5 tbs. dry mustard
    1/4 cup melted margarine
    1 egg beaten
    4 tbs. wine
    1/2 cup milk

Mix ingredients, simmer about 10 min. Careful not to burn.

Cajun Marinade

    1 tbs. lime juice
    1/2 tsp. garlic powder
    1/2 tsp. onion powder
    1/4 tsp. thyme leaves, crushed
    1/4 tsp. salt
    1/8 to 1/4 tsp. ground red pepper
    1/8 tsp. ground black pepper

Mix all ingredients.

Pesto With A Southern Bite

    1-1/2 to 2 cup basil leaves
    1-1/2 to 2 cups collard greens
    3 cloves garlic
    2 oz. parsley
    3/4 cup olive oil
    1 cup grated Italian cheese
    salt and pepper to taste

In food processor, chop first four ingredients. To this mixture add olive oil, cheese, salt, and pepper. Pesto can be served as is over noodles, chicken, and fish, or heated in frying pan, then poured over food items.

Pesto with Pecans

    2 cups fresh basil
    5 cloves garlic
    1/3 cup chopped pecans
    3/4 cup grated Parmesan cheese
    3/4 cup olive oil

In food processor blend basil, garlic, and nuts. Place in mixing bowl. Add cheese and oil. Mix well. Serve over noodles.

Salsa

    4 large, ripe tomatoes, chopped
    1 large onion, chopped
    5 or 6 chili peppers, chopped
    1/2 cup taco sauce
    1 oz. fresh chopped cilantro

Mix all ingredients. Chill about 30 min. before serving.

Guacamole

    3 avocados
    1 lemon (juice)
    1/2 tbs. mayonnaise
    1 med. onion, diced

Cut avocados in half and pit. Slice and peel, place into bowl, then mash them up. Mix in lemon juice, then mayonnaise and onions. If you like it hot, add ground jalapeno. It's also great with diced tomatoes.

Easy Dip

Steam 2 vegetables until tender, then purée. Mix in 1/2 cup sour cream or mayonnaise, 1 chopped shallot, 1/4 tsp. each dry mustard, thyme, and tarragon. Mix. Great with chips or raw vegetables.

Simple Pasta Sauce

In sauce pan melt 1/4 stick margarine, add chopped onions. Sauté. Add 1/2 cup whipping cream and 1/2 tbs. basil and 1/2 cup chicken broth. Cook until thick. Pour over noodles.

Peanut Sauce

In mixing bowl combine 1/4 each creamy peanut butter and plum jam and 1 tbs. each lemon juice and soy sauce. Season with tabasco. Wonderful as vegetable dip or with fruits.

Pineapple and Pecan Spread

        1 cup fresh diced pineapple
        1 cup sugar
        1/2 cup pecans chopped
        3 tbs. mayonnaise

In sauce pan add pineapple and its juice, sugar. Cook until thick. Add nuts. Mix and let cool before serving.

Fruits & Vegetables

Melon Pickles

2 cups assorted melons, cut into 1 inch sq.
2 tbs. sugar
1/4 cup white wine
1/4 cup vinegar
1 tsp. each fresh dill, tarragon, and mint, finely chopped

In large bowl, mix wine and vinegar. Add sugar and herbs, mix until sugar is dissolved. Add melons, then chill at least 3 hours before serving.

Zucchini in White Wine Sauce

2 cups zucchini, sliced
1/2 cup sliced onion
2 tbs. margarine
2 tbs. flour
4 oz. cream
1/4 cup Chardonnay
2 tbs. parsley, chopped
1/4 tsp. Worcestershire sauce
season to taste

Steam zucchini and onion about 4 min. In saucepan, melt margarine. Add flour and cream, constantly stirring until smooth. Add half the parsley, and all Worcestershire sauce and seasoning. Add Chardonnay, slowly constantly stirring. Remove from heat. Place vegetables in casserole dish. Cover with wine sauce. Add remaining parsley. Bake in 350 degree oven until bubbly. Add cheese if you care to.

The Way Mama Fries Corn for Three

 5 to 6 ears corn (cut from the cob)
 1/4 cup oil
 1 cup water
 2 tbs. flour
 salt and pepper to taste

In large frying pan. Heat oil (very hot). Mix corn, flour and seasoning, add water. Add to frying pan — if needed, add more water. Fry about 7 mins. Lower heat, let simmer about 30 more min.

Red Beans and Rice

 1 lb. dried red kidney beans
 1 pot water
 2 chicken backs or legs
 1 large onion, chopped
 2 cloves garlic, chopped
 1/4 cup celery, chopped
 1/2 tsp. tabasco
 1 tsp. salt
 1/4 tsp. thyme
 1 bayleaf
 3 cups hot cooked rice

Soak beans in water overnight. Pour into a large pot. Add remaining ingredients, except rice. Simmer about 3 hours, or until beans are tender. Add water when necessary during cooking. Water should just cover beans when cooking ends. Remove 1 cup of the cooked beans and mash into paste. Pour back into pot. Stir until liquid is thickened. Serve over rice.

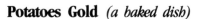

Potatoes Gold *(a baked dish)*
    1 clove garlic, chopped
    2 tbs. margarine
    2-1/2 lbs. potatoes, peeled and sliced very thin
    1/2 cup cream
    1-1/2 cups grated Gruyère cheese
    1/3 cup margarine, cut into small pieces
    salt and pepper

Use a heavy baking dish which can double as the serving dish. Rub bottom and sides with garlic and 2 tbs. margarine. Place half the potatoes in bottom; cover with half the cheese and seasoning. Dot with margarine. Cover that with remaining potatoes, then last of the cheese. Pour cream into side of dish around the potatoes. Bake in preheated 400 degree oven until potatoes are golden brown, about 40 min.

Lima Beans And Herbs
    2 lbs. cooked lima beans *(if fresh are not available, use frozen)*
    1/2 cup heavy cream
    3 oz. cooked turkey breast, sliced into thin strips
    2 tbs. fresh chopped parsley
    2 tbs. fresh chopped chervil

In a sauce pan combine turkey and cream. Add salt and pepper. Bring to boil until cream thickens, about 6 min. Place limas in serving dish and keep warm. Add cream with turkey and chopped herbs, then toss and serve.

Haricots Verts *(French beans)*

> 1 lb. French beans *(if not available, use very small green beans)*
> 1 oz. margarine
> 1 med. onion, chopped
> salt and pepper to taste

Cut tops and tails off beans, then cook them in boiling water about 12 min. While beans are cooking, in frying pan fry chopped onions in the margarine until onions are golden brown — not burned. Drain beans and toss to dry. Pour onion and margarine over beans and serve. Season with salt and pepper.

Red Pears

> 2 cups dry red wine
> juice of 1/2 lemon
> 1 strip lemon peel
> 1 small piece of cinnamon
> 6 small Comice pears peeled, with stems left on

In medium pot add wine, lemon juice, peel, sugar, and cinnamon. Bring to a boil, stir to dissolve sugar. Remove eyes from bottom of pears, then add to wine. Lower heat and simmer about 20 min. Be sure wine covers all of the pears. Allow pears to cool in the syrup. Remove cinnamon stick and lemon peel and discard. Place pears in serving dish. Spoon syrup over. Serve warm or chilled.

Zucchini Casserole

    2 zucchini, sliced
    1 onion, sliced
    4 slices bread, broken up
    2 cups milk
    4 large eggs, beaten
    salt and pepper to taste

Steam zucchini and cool. In a casserole dish add zucchini, crumbled bread, milk, and eggs. Bake in 375 degree oven 25 to 30 min.

Greengrocer Stuffed Zucchini

    1 large zucchini
    1/4 lb. ground turkey
    1 small onion, chopped
    2 cloves garlic, chopped
    1/2 pepper, chopped
    1/2 lb. grated cheese
    2 tbs. Worcestershire sauce
    salt and pepper

Slice zucchini about 3/4 inch from blossom end. Take the large portion and core it. Set aside. Combine remaining ingredients. Mix well. Stuff zucchini with turkey mixture. Bake at 425 degrees for about 35 min. Slice into rings. Sprinkle with cheese. Serve.

Stuffed Chayote Squash

    2 Chayote squash
    4 oz. ground turkey
    2 oz. each red, green, and yellow pepper, chopped
    3 oz. onion, chopped
    1 oz. olive oil
    4 oz. grated cheese.

Slice chayote in half. Boil in salty water for about 30 min. Scoop out seeds and discard. Scoop out flesh and mix with other ingredients except cheese. Sauté with olive oil. Stuff sautéed vegetables in squash halves, then bake in 325 degree oven about 20 min. Sprinkle with cheese and serve.

Stuffed Peppers

    1-1/2 cups cooked rice
    1/2 lb. ground turkey
    1 onion, chopped
    1 tsp. salt
    1 carrot, diced
    1/2 cup celery chopped
    5 or 6 cored peppers

Sauté turkey and chopped vegetables. Season and add rice. Stuff into pepper and bake at 350 degrees for about 30 min. Add cheese topping if you like.

Glazed Onions

    15 small onions peeled
    10 tsp. honey
    4 tbs. butter or margarine
    1/2 tsp. salt
    1/4 tsp. pepper

Place onion in baking dish. Add seasoning and butter. Pour honey over. Then bake in 450 degree oven for about one hour.

Asparagus and Parmesan

> 1/2 lb. steamed asparagus
> 3 tbs. margarine melted
> 2 tbs. lemon juice
> 4 tbs. grated Parmesan cheese

In a shallow pan, place asparagus. Pour other ingredients over. Place under broiler for about 3 min. Serve. *You may also use other vegetables as well.*

Mama's Collards

> 1 bunch collards, stemmed, washed very well,
>   and torn into small pieces
> 2 -1/4 cup water
> 2 chicken thighs
> light salt and pepper to taste

Boil chicken about 20 min. Add collards and seasoning. Lower heat, cook about 2 hours or until greens are tender. *HAPPY NEW YEAR!*

Mama's Fried Okra

(You will love it.)

> 2 lbs. okra
> 1/2 cup self-rising corn meal
> 2 tbs. self-rising flour
> 1-1/2 cups oil
> dash salt and pepper

Wash and cut okra into 1/4-inch pieces. Mix corn meal, flour and seasoning. Add okra. Pour oil into deep frying pan and heat to about 400 degrees. Fry okra and corn meal mixture.

Mama's Green Beans

Green beans cut into 1/2 inch pieces
2 cups water
1 tbs. salt
1/4 cup oil

In a pot, boil water. Add salt, oil, and beans. Lower heat and simmer about 1-1/2 hours. During the last 30 min., add peeled and quarted potatoes and pepper if you like.

Mama's Candied Sweet Potatoes

4 sweet potatoes, peeled and sliced
1/2 cups water
1-1/2 cups sugar
1 stick margarine
1 tsp. lemon juice
1 tbs. vanilla

In boiler add water, sweet potatoes, and sugar. Boil. Add margarine, juice, and vanilla. Lower heat after 15 min. Simmer 20 min. longer.

Marinated Mushrooms *(other Veggies can be substituted)*

2 lbs. button mushrooms, washed and trimmed
1 cup olive oil
1/2 cup white wine vinegar
4 tbs. lemon juice
2 bunches green onion, chopped
1/2 cup parsley, chopped
1 oz. fresh tarragon, chopped
2 tsp. salt
2 tsp. sugar

While mushrooms dry, mix all other ingredients, and pour over mushrooms. Cover and refrigerate, at least 1 day ahead.

Stuffed Mushrooms

    15 jumbo mushrooms, washed, stems cut off
    4 tbs. oil
    1 small onion, chopped
    6 oz. ground turkey
    1 oz. Super Sauce *(recipe on p. 151)*
    1 tsp. margarine
    2 oz. bread crumbs

Brush mushrooms with 1/2 the olive oil, set aside. In frying pan, sauté next 3 ingredients with remaining olive oil. Spoon on top of each mushroom. Fry bread crumbs in margarine; place on top of stuffing. Sprinkle with Parmesan cheese. Bake at 425 degrees for about 7 or 8 min.

Ratatouille *(EX-Girlfriend's Dish)*
  1 med. eggplant
  1 each red and green pepper
  1 lb. tomatoes
  1 lb. zucchini
  1 yellow squash
  1 med. Vidalia onion
  2 cloves garlic minced
  1/2 cup oil
  1/4 cup water
  Salt and pepper to taste
  Don't forget thyme — 1 tsp.

   Peel eggplant, squash, and onion. Wash other vegetables and cut every thing into 1/2 inch pieces. Place all in a big pot and add oil and water. *DON'T FORGET SEASONING.* Cook on medium heat 1-1/2 to 2 hours.
   P.S. *She and I are still friends.*

The Perfect Burger *(Vegetarian)*
  1 cup ground walnuts or pecans
  1/2 onion, chopped
  1 rib celery, chopped
  1 carrots, chopped
  1/2 cup seasoned bread crumbs
  1/2 cup cooked rice (brown)
  2 eggs
  salt and pepper to taste

   Sauté onion in margarine until clear. Add celery and carrots. Cook until soft. Cool. Mix with remaining ingredients. Form into patties. Can be fried; however, I feel they come out better when broiled.

Greengrocer Pizza

The Super Sauce
Great for BBQ, Spaghetti, and on Pizza
    3 red ripe tomatoes, diced
    juice of 1/2 lemon
    3 tbs. sugar
    3 oz. yellow mustard
    1/2 red and 1/2 green pepper
    5 cloves garlic
    1 med. onion, diced
    1-1/2 tbs. Worcestershire sauce

Pour first four ingredients in sauce pan. Bring to boil; lower heat. Next ingredients should be chopped very fine or run through a food processor, then added to sauce pan. Next add Worcestershire sauce, and cook on medium heat 30 to 45 min. *If you like it thicker, add 1 tsp. cornstarch.*

Greengrocer Pizza Dough
    1 package yeast
    1/2 tsp. sugar
    3/4 cup warm water
    2 cups flour
    2 tbs. oil
    dash of salt
    1 small onion, diced
    2 cloves garlic, chopped
    2 green onions, chopped
    1 oz. each fresh chopped basil, thyme, and oregano
    Super Sauce *(above)*
    Your favorite cheese

Pour yeast, sugar, and water into small bowl. Let stand 10 min. to prove. Into a large bowl, sift flour and salt; add oil, chopped vegetables, and herbs. If bubbles have formed in the yeast, it has proved. Add it to flour. Mix well with wooden spoon. When dough forms, knead with hands for about 10 min. or until smooth. Place dough in lightly-oiled bowl for about 30 min. It will double in size. Then knead it into a small ball; roll out to fit your pizza pan. Cover with Super Sauce and cheese. Bake in 350 degree oven for about 40 min. or until edges are golden brown.

Deep Dish Pizza Pie

Greengrocer Pizza Dough, to line dish

Filling:

4 oz. grated Parmesan cheese

4 oz. cooked and chopped chicken

2 tomatoes diced

2 oz. mozzarella, diced

1 oz. each fresh chopped parsley and sage

2 eggs beaten

5 tbs. heavy cream

1/8 tsp. nutmeg

salt and pepper

Oil pizza dish, line with dough. Spread half the Parmesan cheese over dough, add chicken and tomatoes. Mix remaining ingredients together. Add to pie. Bake in preheated 375 degree oven 35 to 40 min., or till edges are golden brown.

Greengrocer's Vegetarian Lasagna

9 sheet spinach or plain lasagna pasta
Super Sauce, thickened with 1 tbs. cornstarch
1 lb. ricotta cheese
4 tbs. unsalted margarine
2 cups grated mozzarella
1/8 tsp. nutmeg
salt and pepper

Cook pasta. Drain and set aside. Sauce should be ready. Mix ricotta and margarine together until creamy. Add remaining ingredients and mix. To assemble lasagna, oil baking dish, place 3 sheets of pasta on base, cover with 1/3 of the sauce, carefully spread a layer of the cheese mixture, 3 more pasta sheets, another 1/3 sauce, remaining cheese mixture. Cover that with last 3 pasta sheets. Add last of the Super Sauce.

Cover with foil and bake in preheated 375 degree oven 20 min. Remove foil. Bake about 10 min. more. Let cool about 20 min. before serving.

Pasta with Chicken, Asparagus, and Cream Sauce

10 oz. penne noodles
12 oz. stemmed asparagus, cut into 1-inch pieces
5 oz. sautéed chicken breast, cut into 1-inch pieces
2 tbs. margarine
1 cup heavy cream

Cook noodles in boiling water with 1 tbs. olive oil for about 15 min. Meanwhile, prepare sauce. In sauté pan, melt margarine. Add chicken, asparagus, and cream. Bring to a boil and cook about 5 min. to thicken sauce. Season to taste with salt and pepper. Drain and rinse pasta. Add sauce and serve.

Curtis's Chicken Vegetable Linguini

8 oz. chicken sliced into small pieces
2 tbs. margarine
5 cloves garlic, chopped
1 onion, chopped
1/2 red pepper, chopped
3 tbs. flour
1/2 cup milk
Linguini prepared according to packaged instructions

In a frying pan, add margarine, sauté chicken, garlic, onions and bell pepper until vegetables are tender and all pinkness is out of chicken. Add flour and milk. Cook until sauce thickens and becomes smooth. Now serve over linguini.

Greengrocer's Chicken Dinner

1/2 chicken, cut up
2 tbs. margarine
4 cloves garlic, chopped
1 onion, chopped
1/2 pepper, chopped
1/2 cup seedless grapes, sliced
1/2 cup cantaloupe, sliced into squares
3 oz. maple syrup
salt and pepper to taste

In a frying pan, sauté garlic and onions in margarine. Add chicken and brown. Add pepper, grapes, melon, and seasoning. Place on pan and cook about 25 min. Remove lid and pour syrup over chicken. Cook 10 to 15 min. longer. Serve with rice or baked potato.

One Pan Turkey Dinner

    1 lb. ground turkey
    1 onion sliced
    1 zucchini, sliced
    1 yellow squash, sliced
    5 napa leaves
    season with Jenny's Salad Dressing

Season turkey by mixing in 3 oz. salad dressing. Then form patties and place in frying pan. Cover turkey with sliced vegetables. Place napa on top. Pour 3 oz. dressing over napa. Place lid on pan. Cook on medium heat 25 to 35 min.

Six-Layer Turkey Dinner

    2 lbs. ground turkey, sautéed
    3 oz. honey dill mustard
    3 oz. grain mustard
    1 onion, chopped
    1 Granny Smith apple, chopped
    1 each green and red pepper, chopped
    2 broccoli tops, chopped
    4 tbs. white wine
    1 red apple

Sauté all vegetables in white wine for about 3 min. Cool.

In casserole dish, **layer 1:** 1 lb. ground turkey pressed flat, **layer 2:** honey dill mustard, **layer 3:** vegetables, **layer 4:** 1 lb. turkey, **layer 5:** honey grain mustard, **layer 6:** sliced red apple. Bake in 325 degree oven about 40 min.

Eleneki Chicken *A recipe I learned while vacationing in Hawaii. For a family of 4 Hawaiians (they love to eat).*

Step 1.
 12 chicken thighs, boned and quartered
 32 oz. soy sauce
 3 cups sugar
 3 oz. fresh ginger, grated
 4 cloves garlic, chopped
 2 large, quartered sweet onions

In a large pot, marinate all items for at least 4 hours (overnight is best). Pour off half the liquid (save it, you may need it during cooking). Cook on high heat about 30 min. or until chicken is done.

Step 2. *After chicken is done, lower heat, add to pot:*
 8 oz. canned bamboo shoots (sliced)
 8 oz. long rice (soak 30 min. in warm water)
 2 or 3 bunches green onion (chopped)
 6 oz. fresh mushrooms, sliced
 8 oz. diced tofu
 1 pack abrage (fried tofu) sliced

Cook about 15 min. longer and serve with rice. You will love it.

Papaya Roasted Chicken
 1/2 chicken, cut up
 1 papaya, seeded and diced
 1/2 green pepper, diced
 1/2 onion, diced
 salt and pepper to taste

In a roasting pan, pour half the papaya, then chicken. Smother with remaining ingredients. Roast in 325 degree oven 45 min. (longer if needed)

Tropical Chicken

    2 tbs. margarine
    8 oz. dice chicken
    1 cup diced pineapple
    1/2 bananas sliced
    1 cup diced sweet potato
    1/4 cup Worchestershire sauce
    salt and pepper to taste

Marinate chicken in sauce for about 20 min. Then sauté in margarine, until all pinkness is gone. Add potatoes, cook about 4 min. Add bananas and pineapples. Cook about 2 min. Serve over rice.

Fish with Herb Sauce

    1 lb. button mushrooms, whole
    1 clove garlic, chopped
    3 tsp. olive oil
    juice of 1 lemon
    1 tbs. chopped parsley
    2 tsp. chopped basil
    1 tsp. chopped sage
    4 tsp. white wine mixed with 1/2 tsp. cornstarch
    4 cleaned fish, about 8 oz. each
    2 tsp. bread crumbs
    2 tsp. grated Parmesan cheese

In frying pan add oil, garlic, and mushrooms. Sauté about 2 min. Add herbs, lemon juice, and wine with cornstarch. Bring to a boil; cook until thickens. Set aside. Place fish in shallow oven dish, pour sauce over fish. Sprinkle with bread crumbs and cheese. Cover with foil, not too tight, and cook in preheated 375 degree oven about 20 min. Remove foil last 5 min. of cooking.

Tropical Cheesecake

Making this cake is fun; there are three separate parts which must be combined.

Pineapple Glaze

2-1/2 cups pineapple, diced
1/3 cup sugar
1/3 cup water
1 tbs. cornstarch

In a small sauce pan, add pineapple, sugar, and water. Bring to boil. Lower heat and add cornstarch, stirring constantly until thickened. This glaze is not only good over cheesecake; try it over ice cream, sliced fruit, or toast.

Cheesecake Filling

8 oz. cream cheese
1/3 cup powdered sugar
1 tsp. vanilla
16 oz. whipped topping

In mixing bowl, add cheese and whip until fluffy; add sugar and whipped topping. Mix till fluffy.

Fill pie shell to top with pineapple glaze and refrigerate. It will be ready to serve in about 30 min.

Macadamia Nut Pie Crust

1 cup flour
1 stick margarine
1/4 cup sugar
1/2 cup chopped macadamia nuts

In a large mixing bowl, add all ingredients, cut with pastry knife until everything is mixed (what I call a dry stickie). Place dough in pie pan. Smooth evenly. Bake 20 to 30 min. at 350 degrees, or until edges are light brown.

City and Country Kiwi Dessert

    6 peaches, peeled and sliced
    4 kiwi, peeled and sliced
    1 cup fresh orange juice
    4 oz. wine

Place all ingredients in a large bowl. Cover and chill about 8 hours before serving. Excellent alone or over vanilla ice cream.

Peaches Stuffed with Chocolate

    4 large peaches, peeled, sliced in half,
      and stone removed
    1 cup dry white wine
    2 tbs. brandy
    2 packs soft semi-sweet chocolate
    1 egg yolk
    1 tbs. ground almonds
    1 tbs. peach liqueur
    1/2 cup heavy cream
    4 vanilla wafers

In a large bowl, place peaches. Add wine, brandy, and enough water to cover the peaches. Marinate for an hour. Mix chocolate and egg yolk well; add peach liqueur. Whip the cream and fold into chocolate along with the ground almonds.

Remove peaches from marinade and place them in serving dish. Spoon chocolate mixture in center of peach and top. Place wafer in center. Chill and serve.

Grand Marnier Pecan Topping
    1 cup pecans marinated in Grand Marnier
    1/4 stick margarine
    1/4 cup water
    1/4 cup sugar

To sauce pan add margarine and pecans. Sauté about 40 seconds. Add water and sugar and bring to a boil. Stir until mixture thickens. Add Grand Marnier. Cook on high heat about 30 seconds more. Serve over ice cream or cake.

Mama's Pastry Dough
    1-1/2 cups flour
    1/2 cup vegetable shortening
    1/2 cup cold water

In a mixing bowl sift flour, add shortening and water in small amounts until dough forms. Knead until smooth. Refrigerate until needed.

Mama's Sweet Potato Pie
Makes 2 pies
    3 large sweet potatoes, peeled sliced and boiled
    2 sticks margarine
    1-1/2 cups sugar
    4 eggs, well beaten
    1/2 cup butter milk
    1 tsp. vanilla
    2 homemade pie crusts

Mash sweet potatoes with margarine while hot. Add sugar mix and eggs, and mix well, Add milk and vanilla, then mix. Pour custard into pie crust. Bake in preheated 300 degree oven for 1 hour.

Mama Laura Aikens' Pumpkin Pie

2 cups cooked and mashed pumpkin
1 cup sugar
1/2 stick margarine
3 eggs beatened
1/2 cup buttermilk
1 tbs. vanilla flavor
1 tsp. nutmeg
1 tsp. cinnamon
1/2 tsp. fresh lemon juice
1 homemade deep dish pie crust

Mix all ingredients well and add to pie crust. Then bake in preheated 350 degree oven for 1 hour. Cool, slice, and serve. Add whipped cream if you like.

Fresh Coconut Pie

1 cup sugar
1/2 stick melted margarine
2 tbs. flour
3 eggs
1 tsp. vanilla
1 cup buttermilk
1 cup coconut, grated
1 homemade pie crust

In a mixing bowl add margarine, sugar, flour, eggs, and buttermilk. Mix well. Add coconut and vanilla. Mix, then pour into pie crust. Bake in preheated 300 degree oven for 1 hour. Cool before serving.

Chocolate Banana Pie

4 bananas, mashed
8 oz. vanilla wafer crumbs
2 eggs
1 cup sugar
1 tbs. flour
1 oz. soft unsweet chocolate
2 cups milk
1 tsp. vanilla
1 deep pie crust

To a medium sauce pan add eggs, beat. Add sugar and chocolate. Mix well. Add flour and mix. Add milk and bring to an easy boil. Add vanilla, stir, and remove from heat. Add bananas and wafer crumbs, fold into crust. Freeze before serving.

Mama's Special Banana Pudding

2 to 3 lbs. bananas
1 box vanilla wafers
1 cup sugar
2 tbs. flour
2 eggs
2 cups milk
1 tsp. vanilla

In a large bowl, place one layer of sliced bananas, then a layer of wafers until bowl is filled, making sure top layer is wafer. Set aside.

In a medium boiler, beat eggs, and add sugar. Mix well, then add flour, milk, and vanilla. Bring mixture to a boil, being careful not to burn it as it heats. Pour over bananas and wafers. Chill and serve.

Easy Apple Pie

3 or 4 apples, peeled, cored, and sliced
1 cup sugar
1/4 tsp. nutmeg
1/2 stick margarine
1 homemade pie crust

To crust add apples. Sprinkle sugar and nutmeg over apples. Slice margarine and arrange in pie. Cover with top crust. Prick with a fork. Bake in preheated 375 degree oven 45 to 55 min.

Apple Turnovers

I made these for World Heavyweight Boxing Champ Evander "Real deal" Holyfield in Reno.

Mama's Pastry Dough *(recipe on p. 161)*
2 to 3 lbs. apples, peeled, cored, and sliced
1 tsp. vanilla flavor
1 cup sugar
1/2 tsp. cinnamon
1/2 tsp. nutmeg
1/2 stick margarine

Section dough and roll flat. Combine apples, vanilla, sugar, cinnamon, and nutmeg. Fill dough. Add margarine to each turnover. Fold dough over and close. Bake in 400 degree oven for about 20 min.

Should make four or five nice sized turnovers.

Mama's Simple Peach Cobbler
Made in 8 1/2 x 8 1/2 dish 2" deep
>7 or 8 medium peaches, peeled and sliced
>1 cup sugar
>1 tbs. flour
>2 tbs. vanilla
>1-1/2 cups water
>1/2 stick margarine
>1 homemade crust

To dish add peaches. Pour sugar over, then flour. Add vanilla and water. Mix just a little. Slice margarine and arrange over peaches. Place crust on. Bake in 350 degree over 45 min.

Georgia Peach of a Pie
>1 deep dish pie crust
>3 to 4 lbs. fresh peaches, peeled and sliced
>2 tbs. raw sugar
>1 cup water
>16 oz. cream cheese
>4 tbs. milk
>1/2 tsp. almond extract
>4 tbs. sugar

Bake pie crust until light brown; set aside. In small sauce pan, add peaches, raw sugar, and water. Cook about 6 min. (keep that juice for glaze). Set aside.

Combine cream cheese, milk, almond extract, and sugar. Mix until smooth; spread into pie crust. Cover with peaches, and glaze (glaze recipe follows). Chill and serve.

Glaze: Combine 1 tbs. cornstarch, 1/4 cup sugar in a sauce pan. Add 1 tbs. lemon juice and 2/3 cup peach juice (from above) stirring over medium heat until clear and thick. Add 1 tbs. margarine; cool and pour over peaches.

E-Z Cranberry Pie

    3-1/2 cups chopped cranberries
    1-1/2 cups sugar
    1-1/2 tbs. flour
    1/4 tsp. salt
    3 tbs. water
    3 tbs. melted butter or margerine
    1 9-inch pie crust and 1 crust for top
      (or Mama's pastry dough, p. 161)

Mix the pie filling, then add to pie crust. Add top crust and prick with fork. Preheat oven to 450 degrees and bake pie 10 min. Lower temperature to 350 degrees. Bake 40 more min.

Macadamia Nut Pie

    3 eggs
    1 cup light corn syrup
    2/3 cup sugar
    1/4 cup melted margarine
    4 tbs. dark rum
    1 tbs. vanilla
    1 cup chopped macadamia nuts
    1 homemade pie crust

Beat together eggs, sugar, syrup, and margarine. Add rum and vanilla mix. Add nuts. Turn into pie crust. Bake at 375 degrees until filling sets about 45 min. Cool and serve.

Sorbet and French Pear

1 basket fresh raspberries
1 oz. honey
juice of 2 oranges
4 comice pears
2 cup fresh diced mixed fruits

Pour berries and honey into blender and purée. Pour into sauce pan and heat. Peel and core pears; place in boiler. Add orange juice. Bring to a boil. On serving plates arrange diced fruits. Place pear on top. Cover with orange juice. Cover that with the sorbet and serve.

Dessert Pizza

Mama's pastry dough
2 tbs. margarine
3 tbs. brown sugar
papaya sauce or raspberry sorbet
any other fruits as topping

Roll dough and flatten to fit pizza pan. Cover with brown sugar. Then add sauce and other toppings. Bake in preheated 300 degree oven for about 1 hour. Add grated coconut to give a cheese look.

Pineapple Caramel

1 fresh pineapple, sliced and diced
1/3 cup brown sugar
1/3 cup margarine
1/3 cup heavy cream
1/4 cup chopped pecans

In a sauce pan combine margarine, sugar, and cream. Stir over heat until sugar dissolves and mixture thickens, about 3 min. Add pecans. Spoon over pineapples and serve.

Georgia to Georgia Tea Cake

    1 cup margarine
    1/2 cup powdered sugar
    2-1/4 cups flour
    1/4 tsp. salt
    1 tsp. vanilla flavoring
    1/2 cup chopped walnuts
    1/2 cup pecans
    1/2 cup fresh coconut

First cream margarine and sugar. Then add flour, salt, and vanilla. Mix well. Add nuts, then mix. Spread coconut over working space. Roll mixture in coconut until it forms log. Chill.
    Preheat oven to 325 degrees. Cut tea log into 1- to 2-inch pieces. Roll into balls, place on cookie sheet and bake 15 to 19 min. Cover with powdered sugar.

Chocolate Pecan Zucchini Bundt Cake

    3 cups flour
    1-1/2 tsp. baking powder
    1 tsp. baking soda
    1 tsp. salt
    4 eggs
    3 cups sugar
    3 packs soft baking chocolate
    1-1/2 cup oil
    3 cups grated zucchini
    1 cup chopped pecans
    3 tbs. powdered sugar

Mix first 4 ingredients and set aside. In a mixing bowl, beat eggs, add sugar, 1/4 cup at a time. Add chocolate mix, then add oil. Add flour mixture and blend well. Fold in zucchini and pecans. Mix well. Fold into bundt pan. Bake in preheated 350 degree oven for 1 hour and 15 min. Cool 15 min. before removing cake from pan. Sprinkle powdered sugar on cake and serve.

Breadstuffs

Apple Muffins

    3/4 cup cooking oil
    1 cup sugar
    2 eggs
    1-1/2 cups flour
    1 tsp. salt
    1 tsp. baking soda
    1 tsp. vanilla
    1 tsp. cinnamon
    2 apples, peeled and diced

Combine oil, sugar, and egg. Mix well. Blend in flour, salt soda, cinnamon, and vanilla. Pour into muffin pan. Bake at 350 degrees 10 to 15 min.

Orange Muffins

    3/4 cup cooking oil
    1 cup sugar
    2 eggs
    1-1/2 cups flour
    1 tsp. salt
    1 tsp. baking soda
    1 tsp. vanilla
    1/4 cup fresh orange juice
    2 tbs. grated orange rine.

Combine oil, sugar, and eggs. Mix well. Add remaining ingredients. Blend. Pour into muffin pan. Bake at 350 degrees for 10 to 15 min.

Crepes Chocolate with Strawberry Jam
Batter
> 1-1/2 cups milk and water mixed
> 4 eggs
> 1/8 tsp. salt
> 2 cups flour, sifted
> 1 tbs. sugar
> 4 tbs. melted margarine

Filling
> 8 oz. semi-sweet chocolate, grated
> 4 oz. strawberry jam
> whipped cream
> toasted pecans

In a large bowl, add batter ingredients. Mix well until creamy batter forms. To cook: brush crepe or small frying pan with oil over high heat. Add large spoonful of batter. Swirl in pan to cover base. Pour off excess batter. Brown one side, then the other. As crepes are cooked, spread jam and chocolate on one side the fold. Repeat this until all batter is cooked. Makes at least 12 crepes. Divide into serving size. Top with whipped cream and nuts.

Potato Pancakes
> 3 med. raw potatoes
> 1 small onion
> 1 egg
> 2 tbs. flour
> dash of pepper
> 1/2 tsp. salt
> 1/4 tsp. baking powder

Peel and grate potatoes and onion. Let stand 10 to 15 min., then pour off the liquid. Add remaining ingedients and mix well. Drop by spoonfuls into hot oiled skillet and fry three to four min. on each side. Great with apple butter or sour cream.

German Apple Pancakes

    1 cup sifted flour
    1/2 tsp. baking powder
    pinch of salt
    1 cup milk
    5 eggs
    2 tbs. melted butter
    2 med. apples, sliced thin and sautéed in butter

Mix dry ingredients. Stir in milk. Add eggs one at a time and beat into batter. Add melted butter.

Pour in hot oiled skillet. Then bake in 425 degree oven until puffed and golden brown, 20 to 25 min.

Serve hot with sautéed apples on top.

Banana Bread

    2 eggs beaten
    1/2 cup melted margarine
    3 ripe bananas, mashed
    1 cup sugar
    1/2 cup flour
    1/2 tsp. salt
    1 tsp. baking soda
    1-1/2 cups whole wheat flour
    1/2 cup hot water

Mix eggs, margarine, sugar, and bananas. Add 1/2 cup flour. Mix. Add remaining ingredients one at a time, mixing well with each addition until batter has thickened. For Quick Bread, pour in wide pan and bake at 375 degrees for 15 to 20 min. For loaf, pour into loaf pan. Bake 60 min. longer if needed.

Notes

Notes

Notes